The Manager's Guide to Counselling at Work
Michael Reddy

3 Phases

Understand
Challenge
Resolve

THE MANAGER'S GUIDE TO
COUNSELLING AT WORK

BPS

Published by The British Psychological Society and

Methuen
London and New York

MICHAEL REDDY

First published in 1987 by The British Psychological Society, St Andrews House, 48 Princess Road East, Leicester, LE1 7DR in association with Methuen & Co. Ltd., 11 New Fetter Lane, London EC4P 4EE, and in the USA by Methuen, Inc., 29 West 35th Street, New York NY 10001.

British Library Cataloguing in Publication Data

Reddy, Michael
 The manager's guide to counselling at work.
 1. Employee counselling
 I. Title II. British Psychological Society
 658.3'85   HF 5549.5.C8
 ISBN 0-901715-70-0

Set in Garamond by Prestige Filmsetters, Leicester
Printed and bound in Great Britain by
Biddles Ltd, Guildford and King's Lynn

ACKNOWLEDGEMENTS

A number of people from a broad range of management positions and organizations reviewed this text while it was in production. I was surprised at, and all the more grateful for, the thoroughness and care such busy men and women put into their comments. The book is much improved and much tidier for their work. They also rid me of a number of illusions – that I can effortlessly write good English, that I know all about punctuation, spelling and so on.

Those in particular whose contributions were vital are John O'Brien, Francesca Thomas (BBC), Louis Mallet (Foxborough International), Susan Howell, Donald McLean and Coral Morgan-Thomas (The Role Organization), Peter Walker (Texas Instruments), Peter Swift (BPCC), Geoff Powell (Leicestershire County Council), Barry Edwards, Jay Buckingham (TSB Trustcard), Colin McDonald (Metropolitan Police), Ken Sanderson (British Telecom) and Yvonne Wells (North Thames Gas).

As is usual and quite correct I take responsibility for the final version. "Final" is said with a feeling of satisfaction, shared by Liz Dugdale, who typed all the previous versions as well. The feeling is probably shared too by those indefatigable and patient editors at The British Psychological Society, Joyce Collins and Christopher Feeney, but they would never let on.

The long Section Two of this book covers all the main aspects of the skills of counselling. It is designed for all those whose job entails some counselling – whether it be in career direction and manpower deployment, personal problems or performance-related issues. There are others, especially senior managers, who may not involve themselves directly with counselling, but who perceive the strategic contribution it can make to the organization's objectives and want to know more about it. The first three and the last three chapters were written with them in mind.

CONTENTS

1   COUNSELLING AT WORK

*It is becoming a commonplace that people are the most important asset of a
business; that their effective and relatively satisfied functioning can make the
difference between success and failure; that indifference to human resources is
a social problem; and so on.*

*Responsible leaders in personnel and line management have been attracted to
the idea of counselling for both humanitarian and highly practical reasons. It
is humanitarian to recognize that the changing pattern of working life brings
real pressure and hardship to many individuals. It is realistic and entirely
pragmatic to see that counselling may well be the most economical means of
improving performance, given that the quality of work can be so quickly
effected by purely personal factors.*

*This interest is reflected in the creation of new associations, such as the British
Association for Counselling with its Counselling At Work division, which
directly address the need for counselling skills among those involved in day-to-
day contact with and leadership of people in public and private sector
organizations.*

■ ■ ■ ■

WHO WILL FIND THIS BOOK USEFUL?

To date there has been very little written specifically for this sizeable body of
managers and administrators, principals and department heads, who
have to use counselling skills on a daily basis simply to get the best out of
their people. Some of them do it well in a quite intuitive way. Most, however,
would do better with a practical or conceptual framework to guide them.

There are plenty of such texts for teachers, nurses, marriage guidance
counsellors and the like, but not for line and personnel managers. A lot is
now known about the broad processes of counselling wherever it takes
place, but not much of it has percolated into the industrial world, where its
relevance has been suddenly recognized.

This book is written as a means of bridging the gap between what the experts
are saying and what managers have to *do* every day.

Managers and administrators are of course not the only ones to be involved
in counselling. I have as clearly in mind the personnel, training and welfare
officer, the union representative and the occupational nurse. Some of the

examples involve simply a sympathetic colleague. The basic principles of counselling are the same in every case.

> Somebody called it 'corridor conversations' – a slight exaggeration but it does underline the fact that a lot of good counselling and helping is done in passing, does not need to take long, does not have to be in a formal setting and does not require a degree to do it.

AM I SUPPOSED TO BE A PSYCHOLOGIST THEN?

There are times when people need professional help and I would do no one a service by proposing that the working manager or work colleague should try to substitute for it. What I am proposing is something rather different:

☐ 1. There is a difference between using counselling skills and being a counsellor. This book is about the former. It illustrates from time to time how professional counsellors work and think, because their perspective is necessary for an understanding of the full range of skills. But skills are what I have in view, and their use by the generic, non-professional counsellor in an organization, typically a manager.

☐ 2. Such a person is often best placed to spot the individual with a problem, best placed perhaps to bring to bear a little pressure towards finding a solution; sometimes in the best position to *do* something about it or at the very least to guide people to the help they need.

☐ 3. The working manager or colleague can intervene in a number of daily situations which *may* call for professional help, but which may equally be satisfied by a little informal counselling of the kind described here. Indeed, there are some situations where a timely and early move by the boss/colleague can forestall the need for professional help, and incidentally release lost energy back into the organization. There are several such examples throughout the book.

Very often this simply does not happen because neither makes a move. The person with a problem (like most of us with a toothache) hopes it will simply go away. The manager or colleague, however willing, is often unsure *how* to engage in this role, and has perhaps wisely thought he or she might do more damage and refrains from offering a word. But it is now possible, in a way which was not the case until relatively recently, to offer practical guidelines to those who are willing to help.

THE MANAGER WHO IS RELUCTANT

Some are *not* willing, of course. They hesitate for a number of reasons:

- [ ] they fear that their assessing/controlling role will be undermined
- [ ] they believe that a show of sympathy on their part will be exploited by subordinates
- [ ] they think that being sympathetic with a person means they cannot make any further demands on him or her
- [ ] they say that their job description doesn't include "social work"
- [ ] they say they simply don't have time.

For those who are truly and fundamentally resistant to taking on the counselling role, even for a limited time, the best advice is: *DON'T.*

Yet, in the form in which they are usually expressed these objections and apprehensions are misplaced. Time, for example, is not really a factor. Any time spent in counselling a subordinate is not likely to be long and will probably be repaid several times over in terms of increased productivity and motivation.

Leadership and management are both said to hinge on the desire and ability to make other people successful. The skills of counselling are a sub-set of the skills of leadership. They may not be deployed every day but one timely intervention by a respected boss or colleague can make a difference to an individual which will stay with them for the rest of their life.

COMMON MISTAKES

Apart from those who are *unwilling* to be involved with subordinates on anything other than work and performance issues, there are others who would like to help but may not know how, or who are under some misapprehensions about what counselling actually means. They may be nervous that if they allow a person to "open up", he or she might suddenly become emotional – and then what? What would they do?

And then maybe nothing, is the answer. It may be that allowing someone to release a pent-up feeling is the one piece of help no one else was able to give. With the storm blown out, reason and clearer thinking often reassert themselves with surprising speed. The "counsellor" has only to let it happen.

There are other typical apprehensions and mistakes which hold back some managers from offering help when they are best placed to offer it:

- [ ] they plunge into talking about themselves with the idea that this will help: it probably won't

- [ ] they set about cheering the other person up: this can be doubly depressing

- [ ] they move straight into the solution mode: understandable – but too soon

- [ ] they think that help necessarily means *DOING* something for a person: often it doesn't

- [ ] they believe that at the very least they will need to find a piece of cogent advice: not necessarily.

What are they supposed to do then? Is there anything left? What is left is the essence of counselling and helping.

SECTION ONE
What Counselling Is and How It Helps

Chapter 2 gives the background to the current interest in counselling and the research which has shaped and directed it.

Chapter 3 outlines the process of counselling, breaking it down into its three characteristic phases.

Chapter 4 looks at two key elements in counselling and the relationship which is implied between "helper" and "client".

2 THE BACKGROUND TO COUNSELLING

This chapter clears the ground by looking at the research which makes a book like this possible, then goes on to a definition of counselling, a sketch of the individual who might benefit from it, and the first brief outline of the counselling process.

■ ■ ■ ■

THE NEW AND THE OLD

What is new about counselling?

First of all, it is not some new invention. Rather, it is something which has always been a part of life and a part of working life.

An introduction to counselling for anybody (managers included) should show that they have already experienced it, from both sides. That is, they have counselled and been counselled. Counselling is not totally new to them. It might not have carried the name, but it is as much a part of organizational life as quality control and cashflow. Its purpose is to help people through periods and problems which affect their satisfaction and performance on the job.

> As well as being of great benefit to the individual, the results of counselling should show up on the bottom line, just like the results of good selection procedures, good marketing strategies and the rest.

If counselling itself is not something new, what is recent (though it has been going on now for some 50 years) is a series of observations and research projects which have isolated the key ingredients in good counselling. We can now say what counselling is, what it looks like, how it works.

Conversely, we can now say what has happened when it does not work. Counselling may be something people do naturally (like raising children or making love) but they do not necessarily do it well. The reason is the same in all three cases: it is not just a matter of technique, it involves the individual as a person.

It is now possible to say, in a way which was not possible until fairly recently, just what makes the difference between good and bad counselling. This book could hardly have been written before the 1980s. It belongs also to a new strain in psychology which is sometimes dubbed "giving psychology away". That is, a movement to de-mystify psychology, to make it available to non-specialists, to pass on the know-how which can be used by anybody.

No, not anybody. Something which is so much a part of daily life should not be left solely to the experts and the specialists. Yet not everyone can be immediately trusted to be a good counsellor. One of the surprising research discoveries is that poor counselling can actually do damage. Counsellors need to know what they are doing.

What is counselling?

Counselling is here defined as:

1. **A set of techniques, skills and attitudes ...**
2. **to help people manage their own problems ...**
3. **using their own resources.**

1. **A set of techniques, skills and attitudes ...** It is the *blend* of attitude and skill which makes counselling such a potent force.

2. **... to help people manage their own problems ...** The approach suggested in this book is oriented round the management of *problems,* in the sense of problems which affect performance at work, whether they be those which arise at work or those which start as more personal problems and spill over into work.

An alternative model might have been proposed, not in terms of problem-management, but in terms of 'helping people to live more effectively', 'personal growth' or some such phrase. This has the advantage of highlighting the fact that counselling does not necessarily deal only with what is *wrong,* but also with opportunities for development and high level performance. Career counselling and management development (sometimes) share this perspective.

Nevertheless, an orientation towards problem-solving is more characteristic of organizational thinking than is personal growth, and, in any case, problems are often the spur to thinking about growth.

Also, I have used the phrase "manage problems" rather than "solve" them. The reason is that some counselling and problem-solving approaches implicitly suggest that all problems can be solved. To take an extreme case, the only acceptable *solution* for someone terminally ill with cancer would be a cure. In harsh reality the problem can only be managed.

Similarly, in a job situation, an individual might be quite tense or upset when he or she has to work with a particular supervisor or partner. Neither of them is going to change to any great extent and neither is going to leave the job. Again, it is a problem which may have to be lived with, managed rather than solved. According to one thirteenth century divine, incidentally, just knowing which problems can be solved and which have to be merely managed is the beginning of wisdom.

3. . . . using their own resources. The central value built into all counselling approaches is that, wherever possible, personal problems are best managed by the person concerned. Advice, coaching and information services are not in themselves counselling, but, rather, complementary and often necessary ingredients. Such services are not wholly separate from counselling. Indeed, they will often be particularly useful to an individual when they are embedded in a counselling approach.

When I say ". . . using their own resources", I mean as far as is possible, of course. Some problems arise from the fact that the person does not *have* the necessary resources, in which case these need to be supplied. But the definition is intended to counteract the typical tendency of inexperienced counsellors to leap in and *DO* something for the person, as though it must always be a question of a lack of resources. As often as not, this simply gives the counsellor more work and misses the point. What people very often need is help to mobilize their own energies, clear their clouded thinking and bring into play their own resources. This is the special emphasis of counselling.

WHO CAN BENEFIT FROM COUNSELLING?

 Derek is a sales engineer (the lifeblood of many a company) and has been with his department for seven years. There has never been a problem – until recently. In the last six weeks his manager has been called twice by important clients with the complaint that he has been abrasive. He has also been moody with the rest of the team for some two months and has managed to reduce one of the secretaries to tears.

It was his manager, in fact, who approached a counsellor. Should he institute disciplinary procedures? The answer, of course, is no. The sharp change in Derek's behaviour is enough to indicate he needs counselling first. Maybe his manager needs counselling, but that question wasn't asked.

People need counselling when:

- ☐ they are not mobilizing their energies
- ☐ they are not solving problems which they have the resources to solve
- ☐ their thinking is clouded
- ☐ they are not making a necessary decision
- ☐ they are not responding to usual motivators
- ☐ they are engaging in self-defeating behaviour
- ☐ they are unusually troubled, tense or anxious
- ☐ there is a noticeable change in behaviour
- ☐ they seem unaware of the consequences of their behaviour

Most of us, at one time or another, would benefit from counselling. It follows too that most of us probably work closely with someone who would benefit from it.

COUNSELLING: ITS PHASES IN OUTLINE

The whole of what follows is structured round a single idea: that *all* helping and all counsellors when they are dealing with someone's problem go through three phases.

The Three Phases of Counselling

Phase	Counsellor's task	Client's task
I	UNDERSTANDING	
	... which leads to	Defining the problem
II	CHALLENGING	
	... which leads to	Re-defining the problem
III	RESOURCING	
	... which leads to	Managing the problem

This will be true for doctors, dentists, case workers, charge hands, counsellors and managing directors. There are no exceptions. Only the emphasis may be different.

Another way of putting it is this: people need three different kinds of help, and they need one or the other at different times. Consequently, it is of no use to be offered the wrong kind of help, or help at the wrong time.

I could have called them "aspects" of counselling and helping but "phases" is better because they usually follow in sequence, with a natural place to start and finish each phase. Where there is a personal aspect to the problem, not simply a service to be provided, this sequence will be particularly important. There are situations where trying to challenge or to offer immediate help and advice will backfire if the previous phase or phases have been ignored. On the other hand, when one starts at the beginning it quite often turns out that the first phase is all the person really needs. So that respect for this natural sequence already makes for more effective counselling.

Self-counselling

People actually go through the same sequence when they try to solve problems themselves. They follow the same route.

First, they *define* the problem:

> *"There is simply nowhere I can go in this company"*
>
> *(Phase I)*

Typically the problem is initially defined in a way that makes it insoluble. That may be the precise reason why it is still a problem. Either all solutions are unworkable, or someone else is seen as responsible for the problem, and therefore for its solution. ("He's getting at me the whole time, just picking on me".)

Next, they *change* the picture with some new aspect:

> *"Unless I can get some long-term training"*
>
> *(Phase II)*

Something prompts them to a new way of looking at the situation, to *redefine* it. There is light at the end of the tunnel. They might have been tackling the wrong problem or tackling it from the wrong angle. But now there is a way forward, a goal can be determined, and it only remains to find the *means:*

> *"Why don't I go over and see the training manager?"*
>
> *(Phase III)*

In this case the training manager is the one to help with providing the means. In another case it might be the individual's own job to organize the means. Whichever it is, the third phase is always about *resources*.

Similarly, the three phases the counsellor goes through, with the client, are:

PHASE I: *understand* and make clear the problem as it currently appears.

PHASE II: *challenge* the client to restate the problem in a way that allows a solution to be found.

PHASE III: give the client whatever *resource or help* is still needed to put the solution into practice.

The counsellor, by the way, does not necessarily go through all three phases with the client. Often the first phase by itself is enough. Which is another good reason for starting at the beginning.

> This is not a theoretical framework in the sense that someone sat down and thought how wonderful it would be if things worked out in such a neat and orderly way. It is, rather, the fruit of countless observations and experiments which all point in the same direction: when people are successful in helping other people, this is what actually *HAPPENS*.

Conversely, when it does not happen, one can usually see immediately why not.

Summary

The research of the last 50 years has enabled us to isolate the elements of good counselling in a way not previously possible. By way of introduction we have looked at three aspects of counselling – a definition, a pen-portrait of the natural client for counselling and a sketch of the typical sequence of counselling.

In the next chapter we take up this basic outline and sequence in more detail.

3   THE THREE PHASES OF COUNSELLING

This chapter surveys the whole of the counselling process from beginning to end, and picks out the essential aspect of each of the three main phases.

■ ■ ■ ■

The Three Phases of Counselling

Phase	Counsellor's task	Client's task
I	UNDERSTANDING ... which leads to	Defining the problem
II	CHALLENGING ... which leads to	Re-defining the problem
III	RESOURCING ... which leads to	Managing the problem

SORTING OUT THE PHASES

Breaking down the process like this is not intended to produce a set of hard and fast rules for the counsellor. Doubtless there are brilliant counsellors who flout all of them. Just as there are good golfers who do not swing correctly and good pianists whose fingering is eccentric. All of us can bend the rules from time to time, trust our intuition when it is strong, and come up smiling.

In any case, because counselling is such a personal thing, the counsellor needs to have mastered the method, not vice versa.

And yet, the fact remains that each phase represents a quite different approach to the problem, and at any one time the right approach will be the one which is right for the *client*. Hence the value to the counsellor of knowing what each phase can achieve, and which to try first.

I have seen it often enough – when counsellors gloss lightly over Phase I they may have to start all over again; if they have not lost the client in the meantime. It is quite common that even when the process goes smoothly, the counsellor is brought back again to Phase I as the client brings in new material or wants to test again how well the counsellor really understands.

Before examining more closely the three phases of counselling, some brief examples show the breakdown clearly, starting with the one we glanced at in Chapter 1.

Example 1

Phase I. *"There is simply nowhere I can go in this company."*   Typically, the problem is defined in a way that defies solution.

Phase II. *"Unless of course I get some long-term training."*   A new element changes the picture and makes a goal possible.

Phase III. *"Why don't I go and see my boss and talk it over with him first."*   Action proposed and determined.

□ □ □ □

Example 2

Phase I. *"He's getting at me the whole time. Everybody says he picks on me."*   Somebody else is making the situation impossible.

Phase II. *"Serve him right if I went over to another section."*   A new perspective opens up new solutions.

Phase III. *"Can you do that – I mean, go over to another section?"*   Only needs help now in implementing a solution.

□ □ □ □

Example 3

Phase I.	*"I'm too muddled even to talk about it."*	There is always confusion to start with, about one thing or another.
Phase II.	*"If only I could talk to my mother, but I can't. So who?"*	A new idea – there might be someone else; action is *possible.*
Phase III.	*"Do you know of a family planning clinic or something like that?"*	Now only short of resources to take a positive step.

☐ ☐ ☐ ☐

What I have illustrated here is how people typically counsel *themselves.* The three phases are more or less clearly defined:

☐ I: The problem is insoluble, either because defined as such, or because only someone else can solve it, or because of confusion. *The problem needs defining.* It is not always obvious. People do not always come with a clear statement of the problem. It is the combined effort of the counsellor to understand, and of the client to explain, which can suddenly reveal where the client has become stuck. That may be all that is wanted.

☐ II: Some new element or new perspective changes the overall picture, and allows a goal to be set. *The problem needs redefining.* Now that the problem is isolated it may need to be re-examined. The pieces may need to be shaken up till they settle into a constructive foward-looking pattern. The counsellor may need to do no more.

☐ III: The person moves into looking at how the goal can be attained, looks at alternatives, checks resources. *The problem can be managed.* There may be more work to be done. The client may still need some help with it, until the whole process is completed.

In the examples given the person is acting without a counsellor (which is the way most people solve their problems most of the time, perhaps checking informally with a friend or partner). As can be seen from these examples the person is not necessarily doing the best job of it. Even when the process is moving forward a friend or counsellor will enrich it and make it more viable.

THE PHASES IN ACTION

We can now take a closer look at the three phases, and how a helper-counsellor fits in. The rest of the book follows the same pattern, breaking down each phase in a little more detail, looking at techniques and defining the counsellor's contribution.

The framework also allows counsellors to review and assess what they have done with a particular client and, perhaps, to modify their approach.

PHASE I

Phase I for the client is a matter of *CLARIFYING* or *DEFINING* the problem. Clients will rarely have fully explored and explained it properly, even to themselves. Their task now is to make sense of it to someone else.

For the counsellor, correspondingly, Phase I is entirely about *UNDERSTANDING*. Counsellors may be struggling to understand but as long as they make it their sole task, they will make headway. If they try to do something else at the same time (like solve the problem) they are likely to perish.

Understanding

It is a curious ability, this *capacity for understanding,* or empathy as it is technically called. Some people seem to have it when they first come to counselling, some have to work at it. It is not a common form of cleverness. The more common form of cleverness has us listen speedily to what the other person is saying and with quite astonishing rapidity work out what we will say back. We may even have rehearsed it a couple of times to test how we will say it when the other person stops talking. He or she, meantime, imagines we are still listening.

One of the reasons why we are so quick is that we all have well-developed sieves or grids through which we shoot everything we hear, see, touch, smell and taste. We need to do this, or in normal circumstances we could not react quickly enough. This is a lightning process we are not usually even aware of.

In counselling we put this automatic sifting system on "hold". Our whole mental effort is focused on understanding how things seem *to the client.* To that extent counselling is not a "normal" situation. It demands a kind of concentration and imaginative effort which absorbs the counsellor. Some counsellors seem to be so absorbed they almost enter another world. Which, in a sense, they do, because they have learned this ability to briefly come out of their own.

Such people may be exceptional or highly practised. Yet, at an ordinary level, something of the same sort is the starting-point for anyone who offers counselling to another — some sort of temporary suspension of their habitual scheme of judgment and assessment.

Suspending judgment

How can a manager suspend judgment? Most of what a manager or supervisor does with subordinates is in some way connected with monitoring and assessing (judging) performance, isn't it?

Or is it? I doubt if most managers would see the largest part of their relations with subordinates as controlling performance. They would be far more likely to say *motivating* people was their usual reason for talking to them — and motivating people is not simply about talking and influencing. It includes understanding them.

There are, of course, genuine role conflicts which managers may experience in counselling, and I return to them in Chapter 19 to look concretely at the problems involved.

In any case, let me recall that these pages are directed not only to managers in a simple line relationship but to a broad range of people in personnel, training, administration, trades unions and occupational health. The term "counsellor" is intended for *anybody* who genuinely feels free enough, at some particular time, to show interest and a willingness to understand someone else's situation or problem *from their point of view;* and to help them solve it.

Nor is a counselling session made up entirely of so-called "understanding" responses alone. That would be artificial and would soon become meaningless. All I am saying for the moment is that even if there were only a sprinkling of such responses, most people's counselling style would improve overnight.

The key point is that clients often do not move forward until they have the sense of being understood. Even the *desire* on the counsellor's part to understand is sometimes enough for the client.

Listening – the paradox

Listening, in the sense used here, is a special kind of *communication* skill, where the content of what the counsellor says is loaded towards understanding the client. It is not a typical discussion, exchange or sharing where each person chips in 50 per cent and looks to get 50 per cent in return.

There are a couple of paradoxes about listening. The first is that it actually involves quite a bit of *talking*. Less talking than the client; but a good listening session sounds like a dialogue, not a monologue from the client punctuated by occasional grunts and questions from the counsellor. Listening is an active skill, not a passive one.

Nor is counselling at all like ordinary daily conversation, where often enough we do not really *want* to hear the other person's point of view. We may even be convinced from the outset that the other party is mistaken. So we naturally employ every tactic we can lay our hands on to show them that what they are saying is nonsense. We present a *different* viewpoint so they can see that what they are saying does not add up.

In counselling, however, the counsellor refrains from challenging the client's picture, until the client is convinced that the counsellor has understood the picture as he or she sees it.

We may even go one step further, entering into the picture with the client, encouraging him to explore the rest of it, to paint in a little more detail . . . until, in the end, *THE CLIENT* suddenly says:

"That's silly, isn't it!"

It is a paradox that the most non-confronting tactic imaginable leads clients to confront themselves; providing it is done genuinely, non-threateningly and without sarcasm.

Accepting

It is a final paradox that clients do not seem to move forward until *they* accept that their starting-point is exactly where they currently stand. Even if that means that they have to *accept* they are stuck. Hence they are not helped by a counsellor who immediately tries to push them. "Come on, let's get you out of your confusion", will not usually move people forward, because their struggle to get out of the confusion has only brought more confusion. On the other hand a simple "You are confused, aren't you", said with understanding and acceptance can bring a wry "I am, aren't I", said almost with a sigh of relief. Once it is acknowledged that the starting-point is confusion, the client is now much more likely to be ready to move out of it.

This is another reason why Phase I is important. It is the time when clients decide whether the relationship with the counsellor is safe enough for them to proceed. One necessary ingredient for this is the counsellor's capacity for understanding and for communicating what he understands.

All of this will be looked at again when we come to break down the components of good listening in the next chapter.

Meantime, to recapitulate, the aim of Phase I is for the counsellor to *UNDERSTAND* how the problem/situation appears to the client; and for the client to be satisfied that the counsellor *DOES* understand.

When Phase I is enough

Sometimes (more often than one might ever imagine) that is all the client needs. Sometimes, in being gently drawn into talking about the problem, clients describe it plainly *to themselves* for the first time.

> *"Yes, that's what it is! I'd never seen it as clearly as that!"*

Putting a name to it has already started the process of solving the problem. The client may not need any more. The sheer definition of a problem, the sheer acquiring of a clear perspective is enough for some people to see what they need to do, and to go ahead and do it.

There is another reason why Phase I may be enough by itself. The client sometimes starts with two ideas. One is: "I've got a problem". And the other: "Nobody is going to be able to understand it."

Then suddenly, along comes this person (the counsellor, friend, colleague, boss) who seems to be able to understand it, make sense of it, accept it as a problem anybody might have. Just this much can be immensely reassuring. "At least I'm not going crazy", thinks the client. "I may have a problem, but I'm not weird on top of it." And with that he departs and gets on with solving the problem himself. The counsellor never sees him again.

Where to start and where to finish counselling is a tactical decision with each client. But a few handy rules-of-thumb are:

- ☐ Always try Phase I first.
- ☐ Push ahead as soon as there is an opening.
- ☐ Finish as soon as the client can do the rest.

So far, we have looked at Phase I and shown how it is often enough. Sometimes, however, counsellors forget that there are three aspects to the counselling process, not just one. The aim is not to squeeze every last drop out of Phase I but to push on as soon as there is a way forward and then return to Phase I if the client needs it.

PHASE II

One reason for not listening indefinitely is that there comes a point when it does not help any more. It helps for a lot longer than one might imagine, but once the counsellor begins to turn around in the same ever-decreasing circles as the client, then it is time to move on. It might be time to move on to another counsellor, if nothing else.

Still, the more common fault is trying to move along too quickly rather than stay listening too long. Most untrained counsellors will try to push into Phase II too early in the game. Things like:

> *"Well, I wouldn't worry too much if I were you. It'll come out right, you'll see."*

> *"Oh, don't pay any attention to HER! You know what she's like. No better than she should be, if you ask me."*

The point is not that there is something wrong with the words. They are natural, sympathetic, and may help. The odd thing is they often do not. Why? Because they seem to come from someone who does not understand. If I am feeling upset and someone tells me "not to worry", I may think: "She doesn't understand, or she wouldn't say that."

Such words work best a little later, when the client is more open, is satisfied that the counsellor fully understands, and becomes more willing to listen in turn, more willing to try a new angle.

The aim of Phase II

The main objective of Phase II is to achieve a *SHIFT IN THINKING*. We have all experienced it. We have been in a thoroughly bad mood, feeling badly done by, overworked, unappreciated. Then suddenly there is a stirring television programme. We find ourselves moved, excited or chastened, as we watch someone deal bravely with a difficult situation, much worse than our own. We melt. There is a lump in our throats, and we go and make up with everyone, offer apologies all round for our surliness.

The main aim of Phase II then is to provoke a shift in perspective. Sometimes it is to provoke, sometimes to tease. Rarely might it be to persuade, and never to bully. An early attack on the client's perspective, as in the responses quoted earlier, is more likely than not to backfire. One of the most satisfying events for a counsellor is to hear the client say, with a sigh of relief and obvious conviction:

> *"You are quite right, she's simply not the sort of person anyone should pay attention to."*

. . . when the counsellor has said no such thing!

The client has somehow been brought to say it himself. The various ways this can be done are examined in Chapters 11 and 12.

The first key moment in the first phase was when the client realized that he had successfully got someone to understand. That alone can have a dramatic effect on his ability to move forward. In one stroke the client began to believe there *might* be a solution.

The first key moment in the second phase is when it dawns on the client that there may be *ANOTHER* way of looking at the whole matter; that the solution might well lie down a path which was earlier unknown – or blocked.

"Well of course I'm angry about my wife going out to work! Wouldn't you be!" [Then, suddenly remembering] **"I mean if you were a man?"**

"I don't know about that" [laughs]. **"I do know some men who *don't* seem to mind their wives working. The way they talk, it seems to work out fine. But I can see it doesn't for you. You sound as though you might even disapprove of them."**

"Not disapprove but . . . I don't know".

"You see, as a woman I'm naturally in the middle of the road. There are men on one side who think one way, and men who think differently on the other. They both sound sincere when they talk. And they both seem quite sure about it."

"It certainly gets up my nose. I wonder why I feel so strongly . . . ?"

An example of good counselling work. No great drama, no great fireworks, but a neat illustration of how to move a client on in Phase II. He has taken aboard the idea that there are two equally reasonable ways of looking at the issue of working wives. Already, that is a major shift. He has now set out to understand why he feels so strongly about his own view. As he goes on, with some skilful guiding, he will come up against some inconsistencies and weak points in his own thinking. He will come up against his feelings and the way they are complicating the issue. If the guidance is delicate enough he will end up by confronting himself, not by being confronted.

Challenge and confrontation

Meantime, far from being confronting, the counsellor does not even get into an argument. Had she wanted to be confronting (and there are some whose stock-in-trade is high-level confrontation) she could have said:

> *"I'm a working wife myself, but you don't seem to have any trouble coming to see me in working hours!"*

That would have about a one-in-ten chance of doing the trick. He might laugh ruefully and say: "Well, you have a good point there". If the counsellor knows her man well she might just manage to time the blow to perfection. But the chances are greater that he would feel rebuffed, mutter something about that "being different", and the counselling relationship itself would be in for a repair job.

The work of Phase II from the counsellor's point of view is like tapping on a sheet of glass with a hammer, with the aim of producing a few hairline cracks but no actual breaks. It is left to the client to make the breaks in the way he thinks best, which can be quite different from what the counsellor would have expected. There is challenge in virtually everything counsellors do in Phase II. Only rarely will it mean strong confrontation.

The end of Phase II

The end of Phase II comes when there has been a significant enough shift in the client's view of the problem and it has been well enough consolidated for him to say: "Now I can and will do something about it; let's look at some alternatives." He may have had to question and abandon some long-cherished belief, he may have had to simply give up a feeling he had been nourishing for a long time, he might have had to question his own motivation.

Such re-evaluation tends to move in quantum leaps. Progress seems to be slow and grinding. Then suddenly the client announces: "I've been thinking . . ."

Clients may also suddenly decide at this point that they will go ahead under their own steam. Only if this sounds like a familiar piece of self-sabotage should the counsellor object. Usually it will be right to let them go.

Meantime, on the counsellor's side, the work has been one of nudging and edging the client towards this different way of looking at things. It is not at all an "I'm in charge" manoeuvre. It is more like a tug slowly turning an ocean-going tanker around till it points in the right direction. With practice, reflection and support a counsellor can develop this toughness, persistence and gentleness – and in the process discover how effective, not to mention satisfying, such work can be.

PHASE III

While we are with the image of the little tug turning the big liner around, let us take it one stage further. At the beginning of counselling the big ship is wallowing and drifting out of control.

By the end of Phase I she is steady. By the end of Phase II she is pointing in a definite direction, and knows where she is going, but does not know exactly how to get there. That is the work of Phase III.

It may be that the client does not have enough fuel aboard (conviction, courage, optimism) and will need boosting. Or it may be that she does not have a map; has never been to that place before; may perhaps imagine there is only one route when in fact there are several.

Choosing the route

Doris, for example, has a goal but she does not know how to reach it. She may have determined to give up drinking. She now believes it is possible, and really wants to, but what does she actually *DO?*

Will someone like Doris have to start with a drying-out programme? Should she join AA? What can she substitute for alcohol? Would hypnosis help? How can Doris reward herself for achieving her goal? Should she take a tablet which would make her nauseous after a drink? Will she have to give up her current circle of friends? Should she talk with someone who has had experience of giving up alcohol? Are there any books on the subject? How much of all this should she tackle on her own?

A good slice of the beginning of Phase III may be about alternatives, or *OPTIONS* as people call them.

☐ *First,* developing options – it was quite a surprise to this client that there were so many things she could do. She might not have thought of half of them by herself.

☐ *Second,* sifting options. Some could be impracticable, such as the drying-out programme which she could not afford; some would go against her feelings and values, like giving up *all* her previous circle of friends.

☐ *Third,* putting them into action – where, for example, would she find an experienced alcohol counsellor?

☐ *Fourth,* balancing the pros and cons of each of the possible options.

☐ *Fifth,* which should she adopt first? Attend an evening film and discussion of the subject? Try out a nausea-producing pill?

☐ *Sixth,* devising a way of measuring her progress and setting long-range goals and intermediate targets.

Some of Phase III (maybe all of it) clients prefer to do by themselves. Once it is clear in their minds what they have to do, some people rightly say: thank you very much but I can do it myself now I know where I am going. And they are better left to get on with it.

Guide, philosopher and friend

The counselling role broadens considerably in Phase III. Many clients will still need help in one form or another. Some need further guidance and support. Some may need specific directions, or coaching in problem-solving methods and techniques.

The counsellor may have to be prepared for a bit of down-to-earth, pedestrian hand-holding at this point. As well as some encouragement and prodding.

Another thing counsellors may have to give is pure information. They may have to embark on a little research, or give clients the necessary leads to find out for themselves. Where does one get the required information? Who should be referred to next?

Lastly, the counsellor − especially the counsellor-manager or the counsellor-colleague − may be required to actually *DO* something. They may have to go and speak on the client's behalf to someone else. They may have to meet a simple need like helping to write a letter to the authorities.

 A shop steward visits an operative during the recovery period after a serious illness. He listens to his fears and discouragement (Phase I) and then begins to prepare the man for his return to work. He has to get him to adjust to the idea (Phase II) that his previous job will no longer be suitable. When the man does go back he will need a gradual work programme designed to allow him time for readjustment. The steward talks to the man's superintendent and between all three a step-by-step re-entry is set up (Phase III).

Andy has been in a new managerial post for three months and it is clear that he is overwhelmed. He is stressed, irritable, indecisive, and finally goes in to see his boss's boss ready to explode. Part of his problem is that he has not been assigned sufficient resources. The boss listens with enough understanding and sympathy for Andy not to need to be too emotional and says:

"Well, it's clear you need a break to begin with. We can decide later whether or not you stay in the job. I want to keep you, because I wish I had six of you. The last thing I want is you going under. You need a break. I've understood about the lack of resources and I need to do something about that myself."

The manger set himself to understand Andy (Phase I) and gave him time to rethink (Phase II). Meantime he undertook to do some thinking himself and also accepted that he had a role to play at the action stage (Phase III).

The scope of Phase III

These real-life examples incidentally illustrate how the counsellor-manager or the counsellor-colleague can play a wider role in problem-solving than can the independent counsellor. The manager-counsellor may have the power to change things where the independent counsellor does not.

The scope for the counsellor in Phase III is, therefore, quite broad. The philosophy of counselling remains the same: clients should be allowed and encouraged to do everything for themselves that is in their power. Counsellors sometimes take this too far and hold back from doing something *for* the client, which makes the difference between solving or not solving the problem.

It should be added that the "counsellor" in the two previous examples had played the role well *before* they got to Phase III in showing themselves sympathetic (empathetic) listeners at Phase I and by guiding the employee towards a correct definition of the problem and an appropriate goal at Phase II. The shop steward had spent many weekly visits, while the man was still recovering, to establish his own trustworthiness and the man's personal preparation for Phase III.

> Whether it is *guidance, information* or a practical *service*, the work of Phase Three can best be described as *RESOURCING* the solution to the problem, developing valid options and making them work.

Counsellors soon discover for themselves that such resourcing is best offered on the firm basis of the first two phases. The three phases of counselling are an integrated whole. The counsellor needs to be ready for the whole process.

There will be times when they need not go beyond the first phase, or beyond the second. There will be other occasions when they must. This book is about counselling *and* helping. It deals with all three phases.

Summary

This long chapter has looked in some depth at the characteristics of the three stages of the counselling process – the understanding of the first stage, the challenging of the second and the resourcing of the third. We have also shown that the sequence of the stages is important and needs to be respected.

In the central section of the book we look at the different skills of the three phases, beginning with the development of empathy and understanding in the counsellor, and the core skill of active listening. Before that there is a parenthetic comment on the use of the words "counsellor" and "client".

4   "COUNSELLORS" AND "CLIENTS"

In any conceptual system there are issues about the terms used. Two of them are briefly considered here.

■   ■   ■   ■

THE HELPER/COUNSELLOR

In the counselling situation somebody is the *helper* and somebody else is the client. People have leaned over backwards to change the terminology because they (rightly) will not have the world divided into two camps, the helpers and the helped. The approach taken here makes certain assumptions about people in general which deal directly with that issue. These are:

☐ 1. The first broad assumption is that we *ALL* need help with our problem-solving at one time or another.

☐ 2. This leads naturally to the second assumption that we will all, at one time or another, be best placed to offer help to someone else.

☐ 3. Third, it is assumed that when it comes to problems which touch *themselves,* people are not necessarily good at or systematic in the way they deal with them. They benefit from outside assistance. The reason for this is that people's *feelings* are usually involved at some level. The sharper the crisis aspect of the problem, the more intense the feeling is likely to be. And emotion will quickly affect thinking, logic and reason. Another aspect of problem-solving is *creativity,* and people's creativity is not always at its best when faced with a crisis. At its worst, creativity inspired by panic can lead to catastrophe.

☐ 4. The fourth assumption is that some people, when they come for training in counselling, are already better prepared or more suited to being a counsellor. What distinguishes them is not so much age, or intelligence or some particular knowledge-base or qualifications. There is some research evidence, for example, which suggests that window-cleaners and lift-attendants can be trained in good counselling skills every bit as easily as the professional social worker, psychologist or psychiatrist. I have long suspected that on a day-to-day basis some of the best counselling is in the hands of bar-staff, hairdressers and masseurs. What seems to make the biggest difference between good counsellors and bad is a tiny cluster of human qualities which allow them to develop certain skills. There is nothing unusual about these qualities, as we shall see shortly. They must surely exist in some measure in a wide range of people.

☐ 5. A fifth assumption is that training can help such people to counsel better, both in terms of definable skills and definable attitudes.

THE CLIENT

One day someone is going to come up with a better word than "client" for the person helped. For the time being it gets higher marks than "patient" or "helpee" or "counsellee".

In some ways *patient* is the best word, because in its original sense it is the opposite of agent. An agent is someone who does something. A patient is someone who has something done to him or her. It is quite typical of people who seek help with a problem to cast it in terms of "Look what they've done to me" and perhaps genuinely feel acted upon and to that extent helpless. One of the most delicate processes in counselling is the gradual separation of circumstances of which the client is truly the victim from the victim role which a few clients can play to the hilt.

The point here is that this same process can also be described as moving the person into *agent* from patient. Even from the beginning, the counsellor should be looking to the client to contribute to the work, encouraging him or her out of the "patient" role.

This is not simply a fine point or an incidental excursion into Latin. It underlines one of the central values in counselling theory, which is that clients have most of the resources within themselves to solve their problems. The principle that the client's resources must be brought into play at every point is a guiding one.

This principle also ensures that the client is more likely to learn a generally useful approach to solving all problems, not just valuable help with a single case.

SECTION TWO
The Skills of Counselling

PART I.   The First Phase

The first task of the counsellor is only to understand. Nothing more. But it is thanks to the counsellor's efforts to understand that someone begins to give a manageable shape to a problem, puts a *name* to it ("I'm getting older, aren't I? That's what I've go to face."), starts to separate the tangled strands. Sometimes it is a matter of getting behind one admitted problem to another more important issue. Sometimes it is a question of finally admitting it to oneself, admitting it even to another person – who seems to understand it and accept it as a "normal" problem, which can probably be solved. Any of this may be enough to release the client's productive, problem-solving energy again. The counsellor's job may already be finished.

Chapter   5 examines the skill of "active" listening and compares it with other ways of relating and responding to the client.

Chapter   6 deals with respect for the person and his problem – a necessary condition for the counsellor to listen with understanding.

Chapter   7 illustrates the quality of genuineness in the counsellor as another component of what the client needs.

Chapter   8 looks in more detail at the kind of personal qualities in the counsellor which make for better counselling.

Chapter   9 breaks down the skill of active listening into a set of separate techniques.

Chapter 10 gives another extended example of how the active listening technique works, and how it compares with other approaches.

5 ACTIVE LISTENING

The core skill in the initial phase of counselling (and it continues to be important throughout the entire process) is that of active listening. Its purpose is to help the client to talk, to articulate his problem. One should not assume clients have a coherent version in their heads, let alone at the tip of the tongue. Their thinking and feelings about the problem are more likely to be fragmented and blocked. The skill of active listening is that of drawing out the story.

Most people seem spontaneously to engage in questions to do this, but active listening is a much more flexible and varied technique than questioning. I have already said something about it in Chapter 3; here I examine it more fully.

■ ■ ■ ■

Counsellors may well have to do more than listen, but it is still vital that they do listen. In some forms of consultancy it may be possible to cut corners on good listening. In counselling it is the one single factor which makes the difference between good and bad work. It *is* work too. People most naturally assume that listening is the same as keeping quiet but it is a quite active, *responsive* process. Here is an example.

Client

"I've decided I'm not really happy here. I'm going to get another job. Something in engineering. I wouldn't have stuck it here so long if I hadn't spent four long years studying to be a vet. I'm going to make a complete change even though I'll have to start at the bottom again."

Counsellor responses

1. *"You mean what really matters is where you'll be most happy? Even if it means giving up four hard years at college and starting all over again. You sound quite sure about it."*

2. *"Have you had any previous experience in engineering?"*

3. *"Anything that gives you a greater sense of independence, as usual. I know you!"*

4. *"It would be an awful shame to throw away all that work for nothing, you know."*

5. *"You must have had a hard time this last four years. Why don't we get together over the weekend and see if we can cheer you up!"*

The question is, which is the best listening response? Before going on, readers might like to review the five alternatives and place a bet – which one is it?

Now we can go back over the five replies and this time add what is *implicit* in each of them.

Counsellor responses

1. *"You mean what really matters is where you'll be most happy? Even if it means giving up four hard years at college and starting all over again. You sound very determined about it."*

Implicit: *"Did I understand you right?"*

2. *"Have you had any previous experience in engineering?"*

Implicit: *"There is something you may not have thought about."*

3. *"Anything that gives you a greater sense of independence, as usual. I know you!"*

Implicit: *"I can interpret your deeper motives."*

4. *"It would be an awful shame to throw away all that work for nothing, you know."*

Implicit: *"My opinion about what you have said is important."*

5. *"You must have had a hard time this last four years. Why don't we get together over the weekend and see if we can cheer you up!"*

Implicit: *"Now you have told me your problem I am going to do something about it."*

The *first* response is therefore the only true listening response. It seeks to do no more than show understanding.

The listening response

We need to establish a fine balance here. The listening/understanding response may appear too bland initially, the others seem more spontaneous, which indeed they may be. The listening/understanding response does not come naturally for most people, yet initially it will make the most progress. It only says: I think I understand what you are saying, and I accept it at face value. I don't challenge it in any way.

When they first begin to talk about a problem clients may not be altogether clear about things and may not even state the real, or more pressing problem. They may first fly a relatively neutral kite to see how the counsellor reacts.

Being listened to is rarer than people suppose. It often helps beginning counsellors if they can experience being listened to, can sense what it means for them to be really understood in their turn. It helps them recognize how powerful a response it can be and how welcome. If for no other reason than when one first risks telling someone about oneself one has the feeling that "this may sound silly". To discover that it at least seems to make sense to someone else will often liberate the client to talk more freely.

So the first response does nothing more than reassure the client that the counsellor is willing to look at the issue as it appears *to the client*.

The other responses

By contrast the other four responses take a position *outside* the client's perspective, which he will value later on (maybe only fifteen minutes later) but not immediately. The counsellor may well believe the client is not seeing things too clearly, may believe, as in the example given, that engineering would be the worst possible choice. But this would be entirely the wrong time to say so. In any case, counsellors have no guarantee that they are right either. They need to look at different sides of the case and are more likely to get at them through understanding than through challenging. That is what the other responses effectively do, which places them firmly in Phase II.

One of the most valuable spin-offs from counselling research has been the breakdown of the nuts and bolts of *counsellor responses*. Various groupings have been suggested, some breaking down the process into 12 categories, some into as many as 36. The one we are using here is the grandfather of them all, the one originally suggested by Elias Porter. It uses five categories, a more manageable number.

Within this framework the other four responses given above would be called:

2: *A* **PROBING** *or questioning response.*
It implies that the client ought to consider certain aspects which he has not mentioned. Nothing wrong with that in its place. But to launch directly into questioning always runs the risk that the client (especially if over-adaptive, which new clients can sometimes be) will take the questions as part of a standard interrogation and will settle back to answer questions as one would reply to a doctor making a diagnosis. The more so as the counsellor is perceived to be some sort of "expert", a dubious position for the counsellor to get into initially. The danger is also the more likely if the questions are closed (looking for a yes/no answer) as in the example given.

3: *An* **INTERPRETATIVE** *response.*
The implication is that the counsellor sees more deeply into the client's motivation than the client does. Again, the counsellor runs the risk of appearing as an expert, and not only that but an expert on the client.

4: *An* **EVALUATIVE** *response.*
Here the implication is: I will tell you if the way you see things is right or wrong. This is the response which most clearly says that the counsellor is taking up a position outside the client's perspective, and runs the risk of arousing opposition and debate.

5: *A* **SUPPORTIVE** *response.*
With many counsellors this is a very automatic response. The implication is that once the client has stated the problem it is up to the *counsellor* to do something about it. This is the knee-jerk reaction of those who feel that what clients need most is advice, sympathy and solutions.

Is the listening response always best?

It may seem from the above that I am recommending only the *UNDER-STANDING* response. Not at all. The point being made here is that in the first phase of counselling the client needs to be sure above all that the counsellor *wants* and is able to look at the situation as the client sees it.

To put the matter another way, the only point at issue with the other four responses is not that they are wrong but that they are likely to be premature.

They all belong in fact to Phase II of the counselling process: prodding the client into looking at the issue from a *different* point of view.

Trying to Move Too Quickly

We can illustrate the problems with such over-eagerness by looking at likely replies from the client to the counsellor's initial responses, above.

Response 1:

"You mean what really matters is where you'll be most happy? Even if it means giving up four hard years of College and starting all over again. You sound quite sure about it."

"Well I am. I think I've given this job long enough. It's just not me." [Opening up to further understanding.]

Response 2:

"Have you had any previous experience in engineering?"

"Not really. Does that matter?" [The ball back in the counsellor's court, where he doesn't want it just at present.]

Response 3:

"Anything that gives you a greater sense of independence, as usual. I know you!"

"It's got nothing to do with independence!" [Battle lines drawn. Now its a debate, not counselling.]

Response 4:

"It would be an awful shame to throw away all that work for nothing, you know."

"Do you think I don't know that? Anyway it's not all lost." [Same again: the counsellor is seen as representing a contrary viewpoint.]

Response 5:

"You must have had a hard time this last four years. Why don't we get together over the weekend and see if we can cheer you up!"

"Who said I need cheering up! I feel fine." [A too abrupt excursion into feelings. This needs to be handled more tentatively to start with.]

We have been perhaps a little hard on the alternative responses to listening and understanding. They are misplaced rather than wrong. And on the other side there is also a danger that mechanical listening responses, unrelieved by spontaneous reactions, will drive the client quietly crazy. A blend of understanding responses, sympathetic noises and open questions is much better to begin with.

> The reason for being so categorical about the prime importance of listening and understanding is that it usually comes as a genuine surprise to learning counsellors that their responses are so loaded *away* from listening/understanding and towards something else. A quick test with, say, six client statements, and a choice of the five alternatives for each, usually shows one counsellor strongly favouring probing responses, another given mostly towards evaluative or supportive. It is quite a salutary shock. Another surprise for the supportive brigade is that they suddenly begin to see that sympathy is not necessarily empathy.

"Empathy" is the technical term given to an ability to understand accurately what someone else is really saying, *and* to feed it back to their satisfaction.

That is why it is called *ACTIVE* listening. A useful phrase because it underlines the fact, not always appreciated at first, that listening is not a passive process, certainly not a *silent* one, as may be supposed. Empathy includes not only the ability to understand but also the ability to *communicate* that understanding.

The end-point of the first phase of counselling is that the client believes that the counsellor is able and willing to put himself in the client's shoes and see the situation as the client sees it. Perhaps even see it better. In itself that can bring a tremendous sense of liberation and the impetus to go forward. Things suddenly seem less muddled and threatening.

Summary

Active listening (empathy is the technical term) is the primary skill of counselling in Phase I and it continues to be important in the following stages, where it remains as the necessary foundation.

Active listening responses can be compared with other ways of replying to the client – probing, evaluating, interpreting and supporting. Used prematurely these may arouse opposition rather than foster the drawing-out process which is the counsellor's principal tool in Phase I.

There are two other elements of the counsellor's approach in the first phase, but these are as much a matter of attitude as skill. They are included along with empathy as the "necessary and sufficient" conditions for a good counselling relationship. They are respect and genuineness. We look at them next. Later, in Chapter 9, I return to the question of technique.

6   RESPECT

Respect is not so much a skill to be learned (like empathy) but rather an attitude which can be developed and acquired. It is an attitude of openness, a kind of "wait-and-see" stance which, however, is a long way from gullibility. Rather, it is an approach which says "Let's hear the story first and see if we can make sense of it".

■ ■ ■ ■

OPENNESS OF MIND

Although respect is an attitude which can be developed, some people seem to come to counselling already in possession of the ability to keep an open mind, to withhold judgment. They have a natural set of mind which keeps the options open as long as possible and delays final conclusion.

Other people have a mental set which automatically starts moving towards a conclusion as the first evidence begins to come in and which continues this closing-down process the whole time.

These are two natural casts of mind, equally valuable in different ways, but it is the first which is more valuable in the counselling situation. This is the one which most easily translates into respect for the client. It is also, oddly enough, the one which is most likely to bring the client to change. Why? Because it *allows* him or her to change, rather than pushes and thus disarms the resistance which pushing creates.

It has been illustrated many times over the last 30 years in a mass of research and case studies that what helps people change for the better is not so much any theory, knowledge, expertise or authority on the part of the helper, but rather the relationship which the helper is able to create, and which the *client* can then use to solve a problem, take a decision, make a change.

This relationship seems to be characterised on the counsellor's side by three elements – empathy, respect and genuineness – and it is these which are considered the "necessary and sufficient conditions" of effective counselling. We have already looked at empathy under the heading of active listening.

What does respect mean?

What do these numerous researchers mean by "respect"? Carl Rogers, one of the leading researchers, talks of *liking* and *regard*. At some point he talks about "positive regard" and he quotes some studies which seem to indicate that clients improve to the extent that the positive regard is "unconditional".

"Unconditional positive regard" and "non-possessive warmth", which early researchers coined as a synonym, give some useful sense to the background of the concept perhaps, but they could be quickly dismissed as psychobabble and, in practice, *respect* is perfectly adequate.

An earthier sense comes from an acquaintance who keeps pigs. He was talking about a dearth of good stockmen (the people who actually look after the animals) and observed that "you can always tell a good pigman".

"How do you tell a good pigman?" I enquired politely.

"From the number of animals he can treat as individuals", was the reply.

Might not be a bad yardstick for other professions too, I thought.

Respect means that one treats the individual with the consideration that supposes his or her viewpoint is worth listening to. Without that, empathy is strictly impossible. It is difficult to listen to people without bias if one does not first assume they may have something to say. It is also difficult if one cannot tolerate someone behaving and thinking differently from oneself.

The reader who has dealt with children will probably have known the situation where one is just about to visit one's wrath upon them, but first asks for an explanation of their behaviour – not believing there really is one – then at the last second realizing that from the child's perspective it makes more sense than one imagined. It is this minimum of openness which respect or consideration for the other makes possible.

Why respect can be difficult

Some people have said that even this baseline respect is too much of a mental gymnastic, when their job or role in the organization requires them to monitor and evaluate someone else's performance.

My suspicion however is that there is often something else in play, which is a deeply rooted resistance to hearing what another person is saying from the belief and fear that: if I really listen I may have to agree.

There is the fear too that: if I agree, I may appear to have lost.

Most of us have not practised listening to the point where we feel comfortable and unflustered about the risk of losing *our own* point of view. We have mostly learned to argue (there is always a school debating society, never a listening club); to abuse the other side verbally (we are treated nightly to parliamentary, management or union rhetoric); and generally to treating discussion as an intellectual Wimbledon – a matter of banging the ball back across the net and scoring points.

That is why it is such a relief when the barman or the hairdresser seems to take a polite interest in our opinions instead of contradicting them.

Strangely enough, we all usually consider ourselves good listeners, which would imply that there is generally rather a lot of good listening about. Yet we are usually quite surprised when other people give us a careful and attentive hearing – we are not really used to it. Which suggests that perhaps there isn't so much good listening around after all.

The respect, then, which is necessary for effective counselling is that which considers the other person worth listening to. It is a desirable extra if the counselling manager is also able to convey genuine warmth. This is to some extent a matter of style and personality and is out of the manager's immediate control. What is within his or her ability to assess, control and change is an attitude which allows that the other person has a right to think and feel as they do.

It is a peculiarity of many people that they do not change their minds until their opinions are accepted. It is only when you say to such a person "H'm, you may be right", that they will say "Of course I may be wrong". So it is that the basic listening skills and an attitude of openness often act as a release mechanism, a trigger which propels the person being counselled into a new willingness to trust the counsellor, be more honest (with themselves) and get on with solving the problem.

Respect in practical terms

Sincerely to put effort into understanding another person is already offering more respect than many are accustomed to ("or deserve" does someone mutter?). There are other elements of respect towards the client which are implicit in what the counsellor or counselling manager does:

- [ ] the hard work the counsellor often puts in for clients
- [ ] the confidentiality with which one treats their revelations
- [ ] the refusal to manipulate them
- [ ] the pushing towards self-responsibility
- [ ] the refusal to let them become dependent and to turn oneself into a mere crutch.

All these add up to a considerable "gift" to the person being counselled and go far beyond the basic non-judgmental openness which respect implies.

The possibility of manipulation

Lastly, I have been hinting in various ways at something else, something potentially more sinister, which is that the counselling skill of empathy and the basic attitude of respect can be used to manipulate the other person. In interpersonal terms, apparent empathy and respect are powerful and sophisticated tools which *can* be applied cynically. People will put a lot of trust in someone they perceive as trustworthy; they may abandon their normal discretion and leave themselves quite open to being deceived or exploited.

Summary

In this chapter we have looked at the core elements of respect, the minimum openness to the other person's point of view, an acknowledgement that his or her values may be different from one's own, and taking other people seriously enough to try to really understand what they are saying.

There is one other core quality to look for in the counselling manager beyond the capacity to display respect and understanding of others' points of view – that of genuineness.

7   GENUINENESS

Genuineness is of a different order from empathy and respect.

When we were looking at empathy or active listening we were looking at a skill which could be learned. It was shown as a blend of focused and relaxed attention along with the ability to convey understanding to the person opposite. It may be a relatively uncommon skill but it can be dissected and taught like any other.

When we came to respect we were considering an underlying attitude in the counselling manager, an attitude of openness which represents a kind of "wait-and-see" set of mind. it is an attitude which can be acquired and practised.

Finally, when we come to genuineness, we are talking not about a skill such as active listening, not about an underlying attitude or capacity, like openness, but about some aspect of the counselling manager's personality, some quality. It too can be developed, though even more than the acquiring of a new attitude of respect it might require some change in the counsellor as a person.

■ ■ ■ ■

WHAT DOES "GENUINENESS" MEAN?

Perhaps sincerity would be a better word for it, but *genuineness* is used in most of the research literature. In any case the idea is quite straightforward: if a counselling manager is going to listen accurately, if he or she is going to maintain an attitude of openness and suspended judgment, then they cannot *fake* it. It has to be real, it has to be genuine, it must not be a pretence.

Or perhaps it *can* be a pretence, perhaps it can be faked; but then it is not counselling, because counselling presupposes a relationship of trust between the two persons concerned, and faking or pretending would falsify the relationship from the start.

Genuineness, then, in its simplest form means not faking one's interest in and openness towards a person. In a fuller sense it means *being* someone who is genuinely open, does not put on an act, does not have to play a role. We have all come across people who have a special "telephone voice" and who switch back and forth between it and their normal speech. Then there is the doctor's bedside manner, and there are the suitably solemn tones adopted by a variety of professionals from undertakers to head waiters which are intended to reassure clients of the gravity of their considered opinions.

In some situations this may be warranted. The point is that the ideal counsellor puts on no performance, needs no mask.

This is where we need caution, however. For one thing, no manager engaged in counselling an employee can pretend to have no other role. That in itself would be a pretence and when the manager happens to be engaged in counselling a subordinate, his or her manner should not be something altogether different from their style at other times. Genuineness for a counselling manager will include to some extent staying *in* role. What should not be role-*played* are the interest and willingness to understand which counselling requires and which need to be shown.

Summary

Genuineness (simplicity and unpretentiousness) is a core quality and one of the three major prerequisites for the counsellor. The next chapter looks further into a range of personal qualities which make for good counselling.

8   COUNSELLOR QUALITIES

This book goes back and forth between the techniques/skills of counselling and the personal qualities/attitudes of the counsellor. Both are essential. Technique without heart is empty; heart without head blunders around. But what is "heart"? Any number of aspects might be considered, but this chapter focuses on

☐ *tolerance*

☐ *self-knowledge*

☐ *discretion*

☐ *interest in people*

☐ *liking for people.*

■ ■ ■ ■

GODLINESS

In looking at the aspect of genuineness in a counsellor's style I noted that it could not mean exactly the same for a manager as it would for a professional counsellor, though its essential nature could not be compromised.

The same caution may come in handy when we look at the rest of the qualities said to be necessary for a professional counsellor. Taken together these qualities seem more like a preparation for sainthood than for a job; and make one wonder how such people could actually demand money for their services.

Nevertheless a random sampling might give the practising manager enough of a flavour of useful/ideal qualities in counselling to calculate his or her own chances of successfully transplanting them into local management style. These then are some of the ingredients required or recommended by employers and trainers of counsellors:

Analytical ability .. To sift, track and control the flow of information

Judgment .... To know when to suspend it

Patience .... To control one's immediate reactions

Warmth .... To create a safe atmosphere

Alertness .... To note non-verbal signals and discrepancies

Resilience .... To tolerate ambiguity and seeming contraditions

Plainness .... To say what one means

Trustworthiness ... To refuse to gossip

Restraint .... To control the urge to talk about oneself

Concentration ..... To hear what is implied as well as what is said openly

Experience .... Of life, to allow an element of compassion for people

Training .... To supplement commonsense

Self-confidence ..... To allow the client to be in charge sometimes

Courage .... To confront when necessary

Coolness .... To know when to reassure or sympathize and when not

Firmness .... To stop the client focusing responsibility on outside sources

Prudence .... To stay clear of organizational conflicts

Integrity .... To refrain from abusing authority

Creativity .... To shift the focus of solutions

Realism .... To understand organizational, cultural and political factors

Sensitivity .... To connect with others' feelings

A recipe for sanctity but intended as a source for reflection rather than emulation. Indeed one of the wisest things said about the qualities needed for counsellors is that they should start with freedom from the need for perfection.

Having looked at what our celestial counterparts are doing, we turn to a rather shorter list of personal qualities the mundane manager, colleague or friend may need in order to get started.

TOLERANCE

A counsellor may well get started with the *lack of a need for perfection* suggested above. Counsellors need tolerance and a measure of *self-*acceptance if they are ever going to show it to others. Counsellors who like things to be neat and tidy are in for a hard time. People and their personal problems are not generally neat and tidy.

Then again, clients and their behaviour often do not fit into our own patterns of thought or belief or judgment as much as we might like; and the perfectionist counsellor will be easily tempted into evaluative comments rather than understanding ones.

Thirdly, such a person will find it difficult to deal with the lack of clarity and precision in many counselling situations. It may not be clear what the client really needs – or if this is the same as what he says he wants. It may not be clear what our own obligations are towards him or towards others. Again, in retrospect, it may not be clear that we did the right thing. The client may be delighted but we may not be at all sure if what we did was for the best. On the other hand *we* may be sure we did the right thing, but the client is telling us it is not what he wanted.

Engineers, artists, carpenters, gardeners and many others have the satisfaction of seeing the results of their work in a form which allows them to assess and take pleasure in it. Not so for counsellors. Counselling is full of ambiguity and the perfectionist who likes matters to be unambiguous will be wasting a lot of energy.

From a very practical point of view such a counsellor will be unable to listen properly because the chatter in his own head will drown out half of what the client is saying.

Lastly, the need for perfection usually means making as few mistakes as possible – better still, none at all – and this inhibits naturalness, which I rate more highly than perfection in a counsellor. I much prefer counsellors who are not afraid to make mistakes but are quick to realize when they have, and can then rectify the situation, perhaps with an apology if it is appropriate.

Counsellors need to be fairly balanced individuals, sufficiently relaxed in themselves to allow other people to be different; not to be too disturbed by their contradictions, ambivalences and seemingly odd ways of thinking, talking and doing. To be just that secure in oneself means, of course, knowing something about oneself.

SELF-KNOWLEDGE

By self-knowledge I do not mean being endlessly self-analytical. That is a separate career in itself, and I would not recommend it for most counsellors, let alone the average manager or colleague.

I am stressing it here because people sometimes imagine that to embark on counselling they need to know a lot more about people in general. I want to say to them: No, you would do better, to begin with, by knowing a bit more about yourself.

The learning curve should take beginners first through listening skills. In the process they should begin to be aware of their own reactions, to listen *to themselves*; and then gradually to a greater knowledge of people in general. Counselling is in itself a tremendous education in living. Nobody benefits more from counselling than counsellors. This education, however, will come gradually and naturally in its own time. It may be advanced by learning more about various personality theories but this is not the first priority. Knowing about oneself is.

The best starting-point for counsellors is to become involved in counselling, to learn to use themselves as the main tool and then to be aware of how the process is affecting them, and how they can improve.

Counselling can be taxing

This much awareness of oneself is necessary because counselling can be quite a drain on the helper's own emotional and mental resources.

Counsellors, whether they be full-time or those whose leadership or colleague position brings them into the role from time to time, need enough self-awareness to know when they themselves need help. Experience seems to show that they are not necessarily the best at seeking help for themselves, any more than the cobbler has well-shod children. Doctors and nurses are notorious for not taking care of themselves. Anybody engaged in counselling can be greatly helped by having their own resource and support network, not only to discuss the ins-and-outs of particular cases, but also to offload some of their own perplexity, frustration, irritation, excitement and the rest. Some counsellors try to hold it all in. As though only clients have the right to unload, as though clients and counsellors are somehow two different kinds of people.

Poor counselling can be dangerous

To be safe, counsellors need to understand something of their own motivation. They need to know why they enjoy counselling, if they do, and if not, why not. They need to know when they may be indulging themselves. Counsellors are in a powerful position. The more effective they are the more they are a force for good – or ill.

Research seems to indicate that the most damage is done to clients through counsellors who are perceived as emotionally distant and, at the other extreme, those who are (usually unconsciously) serving their own needs – for love, for closeness, for a sense of being needed. With organizations and companies there is also the danger of the client being manipulated or wronged through the counsellor's privileged knowledge.

 Woman executive, attractive and competent, at least on the surface. But her husband has just left her and gone to live with relatives. Her two daughters are giving more than average trouble for their age. And perhaps she has financial problems. Her insight is good but her self-esteem is at rock-bottom and she has next to no support.

Where does she get help? What help does she need? Perhaps if she could develop a bit of backache she could go and see the medical officer or the nurse and talk to them? But would they get to the real problem? Would they have the time?

Any sympathetic listener, even one with personal problems, may quickly, without any conscious malice, seize on her vulnerability. In fact this example belongs with the next, and interlocks menacingly with it.

A middle manager is helping a female colleague who is going through a separation. The manager is smart enough to know he is emotionally involved, that there must be rumours flying around, that he is probably not helping her, that he is suppressing his true feelings for her, etc. But he's always been a real nice guy. He can't just leave her to get on with it, can he? It would tear both of them to shreds, wouldn't it? So what should he do?

He's asking *you* – what should he do? You are a colleague though not in the same reporting line. It all came out suddenly over a lunch-time drink. How can you help him? Can you walk away from him? Perhaps you *ought* to walk away from him? Or perhaps you could best help by dealing with the woman directly – you know her, she would probably listen to you?

Enough to show how the counsellor's motivation can be muddled when he or she has some personal investment in the client.

When a client sees someone as experienced, balanced and with good will, and interested in him, he will put a lot of trust in that person. There is a naive child still buried in most of us. He will then tend to yield to his judgment, believe what he says, have a blind faith in his values, and so on. The more troubled a person is, the more vulnerable. Consequently the more open he is to being exploited, not just financially or sexually, but intellectually, emotionally, politically.

The power of the counsellor

This is overstating the case for most counselling situations, either because the counsellor is not effective enough to generate such a level of trust or because most professionals have been schooled to be aware of such pitfalls and to subscribe to a code of ethics. In any case, most clients still manage to protect themselves to some extent.

All professionals in training have to face at some stage the highly personal question of how to deal with the power which some patients will give them, whether they want it or not. Some trainees thrive on it and need to get the power-hunger out of their systems. Others run a mile at the sight of the power they have in their hands. But as a psychiatrist said to me on one occasion during my own training: "He may never give that much power to anyone ever again to make him better. *Use* it, for his sake."

In the context of the organization these occasions will be rarer but they will arise. When people are troubled, distressed, confused or angry beyond a certain point they will be indiscreet. They will throw caution to the winds and may behave in a way that half an hour later they wish they had not. Anyone in the counsellor role will be the recipient of such indiscretions.

DISCRETION

Thus arises the question of counsellor discretion, which is a topic in itself. Blabbermouths do not make good counsellors, although oddly enough blabbermouths tend to receive more than their share of confidences. There is the ironic little twist that some people (half-) knowlingly confide in a blabbermouth ("Promise you won't tell a soul!") because they (half-) know it will be all over the place in ten minutes. Meanwhile, they are virtuously telling themselves they would never have revealed it had they realized.

The good listener, the good counsellor, the good helper, every bit as much as the blabbermouth, cannot help finding out more than they would really like to know.

 [Barry:] **I'm going in to see Mike tomorrow morning and I'm going to let it all hang out. They may think I'm not pulling my weight but there are a few things they don't know. I don't care if I burst into tears in the process. I may bleed all over his carpet but everybody's going to know I've been in there.**

Barry's counsellor-colleague, in this case, was quite excited by such revelations, though not in any way worried, since he was not himself involved. Mike (the general manager, and two or three echelons higher) was known to shoot from the hip. The fallout from an explosive meeting between him and the notoriously excitable Barry could keep the place buzzing for days.

What does the counsellor-colleague do? Confidentiality is not the issue here. It is already late evening and the balloon is due to go up first thing in the morning.

The problem is what to do with Barry, and, broadly, should he be calmed down or allowed to go ahead?

This is where the counsellor-colleague needs to understand his own motivation. He can easily persuade himself that it is time anyway for Barry and Mike to have their "High Noon" confrontation. Simplest is to say nothing, leave Barry nicely wound up and hope for a good seat at the next day's performance.

There are, even in the counselling profession itself, those who find it stimulating to send clients through interesting minefields ("Why don't you just walk out on him? You know, give him the old heave-ho! Note pinned to the kitchen table – 'By The Time I Get To Phoenix He'll Be Sleeping' sort of routine") and then watch to see where they blow up.

In the event, Barry's colleague was wise enough to mistrust his own motivation, and to talk things through with him. The net result was that Barry blew out his storm the night before, and went in to see Mike in a quiet frame of mind. As it happened, Mike was relatively relaxed that morning and the two had a useful and in the end very productive session.

But Barry's confidant could easily have been less self-aware, could have persuaded himself that a shootout would be good for them both, and left Barry to get on with a self-destruct.

The counsellor needs to keep in the forefront of his mind the question: is this really in the other person's interest, or am I indulging myself, serving my own ends?

INTEREST

One aspect of the counsellor's own needs may be curiosity. In practice, this is more an asset than a handicap. Someone who is to help others needs some curiosity, some *interest* in people. And most counsellors, professional or just those whom everyone likes talking to, soon have their general curiosity satisfied. There is a sort of "pain barrier" which most counsellors go through, when they cry "Enough! I don't want to hear about anybody else's problem ever again. I just don't want to know."

LIKING

Does a counsellor need to *like* people?

 An admin manager in his late thirties, always wanted to get into sales and has now completed a very successful launch of a new outlet, tripling expected first-year sales. The snag? He has just been fired because the company can no longer afford him. He is on his way to see you, the personnel manager.

In your opinion it is all rather harsh. His appraisal (you have seen it) is bland, too bland, it reflects neither positive nor negative in any concrete way. It also seems strange to say he doesn't have sharp-end sales ability, although you can see that a static, maintenance type of sales manager is all that is needed now, more like an order-taker than a salesman.

Keep him on ice till the next launch? But that is two years away and the people involved say they wouldn't work with him again anyway, though he himself is convinced they would. Is it all a matter of personality clash? That is certainly the case with the man's own manager. So do you go and see his manager? Too late, the man is knocking on the door. What are you going to say? You can soon see what puts people off. He has some quite grotesque gestures and facial expressions, his voice is grating and he appears when sitting to be about to take off like a rocketing pheasant.

But you have been trained in counselling skills, so you know what to do. Right?

Liking people (or perhaps better the ability to come to like people) is useful for a counsellor. Some warmth and some instinctive sympathy is a great asset. Not the constant quest for the down-trodden, the sharp nose for every bird with a broken wing, but a combination of interest in and natural respect for others.

One comes back again and again to respect and tolerance as basic to counselling skills. One does not have to *like* the client but one does have to have enough respect to see things as he sees them and take that into account. Liking may help but it is not strictly necessary. What sometimes happens is that a client whom one immediately and instinctively *dis*likes, if treated with enough empathy and respect, may gradually come to be more likeable.

Liking, of course, is different from being emotionally involved with someone, as we have seen. That inevitably makes counselling more difficult, and usually inadvisable.

Summary

Genuineness was the primary quality underlined by research findings. In this chapter other qualities have been singled out – tolerance, self-knowledge, discretion, interest in and liking for people. Doubtless there are others. Commonsense might be one – if only it could be defined. When we come to Phase II we shall see that the counsellor may also need some nerve and in Phase III patience with detail and minutiae.

Good counselling is a blend of techniques and personal attributes. Before we leave Phase I we return to techniques and to a breakdown of practical skills.

9   TECHNIQUES OF PHASE I

Techniques, in the plural, may be a misnomer, in that all of them are aspects of the single process of drawing out, of active listening. But it may be helpful to break the process down, and illustrate what counsellors actually do:

- ☐ *paying attention*
- ☐ *listening to the end of the sentence*
- ☐ *reflecting*
- ☐ *echoing*
- ☐ *incorporating feeling*
- ☐ *checking*
- ☐ *verifying conclusions*
- ☐ *clarifying*
- ☐ *summarizing*
- ☐ *asking for examples*
- ☐ *encouraging*
- ☐ *questioning*
- ☐ *silence.*

All the techniques of Phase I centre around active listening, just as those of Phase II are all aspects of intuitive challenging.

■ ■ ■ ■

BASICS

This is not the sort of book which teaches people how to greet clients, show them to a seat, make them feel welcome. Most people know already that a desk is a barrier, that for informality and a quiet atmosphere chairs should be set at a short distance and at an angle, rather than facing, that the telephone and other interruptions should be barred, that comfort and privacy are important.

These things do need attention, and I still think it discourteous (though many managers continue to do it) to keep a visitor, colleague or subordinate waiting while some piece of paper is being dealt with, before finally offering real acknowledgement of the other person's presence.

Courtesy is important, as is the ability to put the other person at ease. Yet, in the end, making people comfortable is not so much a matter of pure technique but comes best and most naturally from the counsellor's own sense of comfort – which in turn comes naturally from continuing experience.

PAYING ATTENTION

One might imagine too that one would not have to underline *paying attention* as a technique, but experience has shown that some people unintentionally convey more detachment than they realize – until perhaps they see themselves on video. They then see themselves preoccupied with taking notes, scratching, doodling and stretching, offering little eye contact, lolling back, looking *too* relaxed, using a non-committal tone of voice, being silent for long periods.

Active listening is an active process. It requires involvement.

To some extent posture is a matter of style, but it should include more leaning forward than back, more face-on than sideways, openness, good eye contact and being generally relaxed. Apart from that, attention demands a certain concentration – on what the person is saying, rather than on what the counsellor is thinking.

A good discipline for the counsellor is to *listen to the end of the sentence.* Few people do. Words are normally spoken at about 150 words a minute, but the brain can process information at three times that rate. The question is, what does one do with all the extra capacity? Most people are thinking what *they* will say next; counsellors need to train themselves to stay listening.

I know when I have a good counsellor when I hear him or her start to say something – then suddenly stop. And start again:

> *"You said 'maybe . . . '?"*

There had been a clue right at the end of what the other person was saying, perhaps only in a change of tone. And the good counsellor picks it up.

The other techniques, after paying attention and listening to the end of the sentence, are all ways of "drawing out". They all act like a poultice.

Reflecting. As well as reflecting what a person is saying, through a paraphrase or mini-summary, counsellors often say such words in a reflective tone.

> *"So you don't think it's fair to push the supervisor any harder, but if you don't, you can expect trouble from your own boss."*

A reflection should be faithful to what the person has said but not a simple parroting of their own words. Rather it makes the point succinctly in a way which prompts him or her to say: "Yes, and . . . " Or "Yes, because . . . ". Both of these are a sign that the counsellor has been listening. A continuation which starts: "Yes, but . . . " is a dazzling indication that the counsellor has *NOT* been listening accurately.

Some counsellors have a habit of starting such reflections with words like: "If I understand you correctly . . . ", but these phrases soon begin to sound trite. Even worse is: "So what you are *really* saying is . . . ", which implies that the client cannot express himself properly.

And definitely to be expunged from the counsellor's vocabulary is: "I hear what you are saying". It may or may not be true but the client cannot be sure, because the counsellor has not said *what* he understands.

Echoing. Just the last word or two, usually.

> *". . . promised you?"*

There is an implicit question-mark with such an echo which invites the person to amplify what has just been said.

Incorporating feeling. The feeling may or may not have been expressed directly, but it is plainly there.

> *"So, if you push the supervisor harder you may lose her, and if you don't, the boss will be on your back – and you feel trapped."*

The client says: "Yes, that's exactly what I feel, trapped. Damned if I do and damned if I don't. You see . . ." And off he goes again.

Checking. The last two examples are checking techniques, but it can be done more explicitly.

> *"Did you say she promised you?"*

Verifying conclusions. This builds on what the person has said and tries out a logical conclusion.

"So she promised you. But if that was only on certain conditions, it means extra pressure on you as far as keeping your present job is concerned, doesn't it . . .?"

Clarifying. This may be done openly.

"I didn't quite understand that. Were you implying that she was deliberately putting pressure on you?"

Sometimes people new to counselling do not allow themselves to ask such a question because they believe they are supposed to understand things first time round. They are afraid of appearing stupid. But as well as helping them to understand, this also underlines the message to the client: I really *want* to understand this.

Summarizing. An invaluable technique, if only to allow the counsellor to keep track. Many counsellors, when they are learning listening techniques, listen too long to have any chance of keeping the various elements in mind. They need sometimes to interrupt and say:

"So, let me check so far. There is A and B and C and D and E. Right?"

Apart from checking to see if the counsellor is up to date, it also allows the client to go forward on whichever line is more important. It is as though one proffers five ends of a ball of tangled wool and the client picks out the one to pull on next.

In Phase I, when the client is telling the story for the first time, this is a process which may need to be repeated many times. It goes contrary to two opposite tendencies in an inexperienced counsellor – to come in at the first opportunity and go charging down some inviting path; and to keep quiet too long. Too long to be able to keep track of all the detail.

Summarizing is a slow, methodical process which allows the counsellor to keep abreast of different aspects of the problem – and also allows the client to sort out these various aspects, which till now were jumbled. It is also reassuring to clients because, every two minutes or so, there is an echo from the counsellor which allows them to say "Good – he's got that bit". And this usefully serves to slow clients down, because they are sometimes overwhelmed with the complexity of the problem as it appears to them. The gradual slowing down allows them to relax, with the sensation that the complexity can be broken down into manageable bits.

The only time that this process has to be abandoned is when the client comes in with such a head of steam that he has to be allowed to blow out the storm first. Sometimes he feels that he cannot pause till he has spat out some particularly big globule ("so I just walked out and left her"). Then, when he has seen the counsellor's reaction to that, when he has got that bit out of his system, he can start to slow down.

In that case, the counsellor has to wait longer, for 10 minutes or more, before he can begin to backtrack and try to summarize, to break the story into different aspects.

Asking for examples. Another type of question the counsellor may be too afraid to ask. Clients often say things like, "You know . . .?" or "Well, you know what I mean" and the counsellor does not dare to say: "No, I don't".

> *"You say he always seems to be testing you out. You never know when he's playing a trick on you. What would be an example of that?"*

Encouragers. These may be non-verbal (looking suddenly more intent) or verbal ("Uh huh", "Yes . . . ?").

Questions. These have been left to the last because they can be the bane of the new counsellor's early style. Certainly closed questions (the ones which invite a "Yes" or "No" answer) should be avoided at this stage. Questions are better left open – in fact they really serve as another simple form of encourager.

> *"What do you mean by that?"*

> *"Can you say a bit more about that".*

Above all, probing questions on one particular point should be kept to a minimum in the early stages, as should questions which simply serve the counsellor's curiosity:

> *"Is she the one with the blonde hair?"*

Such questions only have the effect of moving clients on to the counsellor's track – which may not be their own.

Silence

(Even the blank space on the page invites you to fill it, doesn't it!)

The single point to keep in mind is that all the active listening techniques in Phase I are meant to draw out the client. Experience has taught me that I will eventually get to know all I need to know and all I can handle – and it will come out more efficiently in the long-run if I give the client his head at the beginning. Every attempt to get at the story in *my* way will slow the process down.

Summary

There are a variety of techniques which counsellors use in the first phase of counselling. Most of them, like simple silence, leave a hanging question-mark in the air, offer a kind of vacuum which the client is invited to fill. They are all aspects of the single technique of active listening which draw out the client to explore the problem further.

The last chapter of this first segment on the skills of counselling offers another practical example of Phase I active listening.

10 PHASE I EXAMPLE

This chapter illustrates the basic responding skills of the first phase of counselling, using an extended example, and compares active listening with other kinds of response.

■ ■ ■ ■

Like any laboratory dissection of a living process it cannot reflect the reality of live human contact, with all its non-verbal, emotional, highly personal content. It may all come out a bit flat on the printed page and the reader will have to guess at some of the tones, gestures, facial expressions and the like. The aim is to reinforce the illustrations given in Chapter 5 and to steer the person who wants to improve counselling skills another yardstick against which to test his or her own normal style of responding. The question to ask in reading through the five variations is: which of these sounds most like me?

■ ■ ■ ■

The situation begins when a member of the administration department wanders into the personnel section. His name is Brian Lavery.

"I was told I was made redundant three weeks ago. I've only just found out you were here to talk to."

Type 1 Response (active listening)

[Counsellor:] *"Yes, of course, please sit down. It sounds almost like 'I've been walking around in a daze this last three weeks.'"*

[Brian:] *"Well, I have. I keep thinking, maybe they'll change their minds. Or it will go away, or something."*

[Counsellor:] *"Like a bad dream . . ."*

[Brian:] *"Yes, except I know I'm awake. I can't face it. I haven't even told my wife yet."* [Silence] *"I've got to, though."*

COMMENTARY

This is a good piece of listening. They quickly reach the first breakthrough point, the matter which has been bothering Brian most – the fact that he has been concealing something from his wife and somehow making their relationship impossible or "unreal", as he later said.

It is not the most important point (which is to tackle the redundancy situation itself) but Brian will not get to grips with that until he has brought his wife into it.

It is a good piece of listening at this early point because it does not push, it pulls. Understanding the problem may possibly require some probing later. But right now it is not a probe which the counsellor needs so much as a poultice.

The most useful techniques at the beginning of a counselling relationship are *drawing out* techniques. They all focus on inviting the client to talk freely and to develop trust in the counsellor, who for the time being takes a back seat. Not detached – on the contrary, interested and showing great attention and a willingness to understand – but not pushing. Not even pushing the client to tell the story in a more ordered way; just *pulling* him to tell it as he best can.

Pacing

At this early stage, above all, one has to let clients dictate the pace. Their thinking may have been confused, obsessive and circular and the helper may have to let them wander round the houses, at least once, to begin with. Brilliant, incisive and logical shortcuts may initially impress the client (or perhaps just the counsellor) but one usually has to pay later for a too rapid initial pace. The client will doggedly come back to an earlier point which has not been properly resolved.

I remember a manager, introduced to this concept, saying quite categorically: "I don't have time to listen". Then, having been persuaded and having tried it out for a month or so, reporting with obvious surprise "It's actually quicker, isn't it?"

It *is* more efficient, as well as saving time in the literal sense. The manager gets to the real issue quicker and can do something about it more effectively. He or she will find out sooner how much or (as often the case) how little the client really needs. Which brings me to another issue.

Responsibility

Apart from time, some counsellors put themselves under another pressure – that of believing that if someone comes with a problem then the only thing they could possibly want is a solution. They may also believe that it is somehow primarily the counsellor's responsibility to provide one; that this is what the counsellor is being "paid for", so to speak.

Now this simply is not true in many cases. A counsellor is not a cure-all. Yes, clients want solutions to problems. What they often do not know is what particular kind of help or how much they need to reach a solution.

Most clients, once they have got what they want from a counsellor, depart. They take the first opportunity to reclaim their "independence" and get on with living. Sometimes all they need is an impartial hearing, the chance to explore something aloud. They resent a counsellor who wants to push them further than they are prepared for – "No thanks, I can manage now."

If I have been a little emphatic about all this, it is because in training and supervising counsellors I have seen the weighty responsibility that beginners take on themselves unnecessarily, and the relief when they realize how much of the burden they can throw off – and the increase of spontaneity and naturalness which returns to them at that point.

Ambiguity

To put it another way: what clients expect of counsellors and what counsellors *think* they expect can be two different things. What clients get out of counselling and what counsellors think their own task is may be two different things. Ask a counsellor what he or she has done for the departing client and they may say: "Well, what we offer such people is a structured way of looking at their problems and assessing their strengths and weaknesses."

Then run after the client, with the same question, and *the client* may say: "Well, I think the main thing they do is they stop you feeling sorry for yourself – which is exactly what I needed." Is that the same thing? Probably not. Does the counsellor realize how his contribution is evaluated? Possibly not. Does it matter? Probably not.

> The harder thing that counsellors have to face is not the burden of responsibility for other people but not knowing sometimes exactly how they are helping someone, or even *if* they are. Counselling isn't an exact science. It isn't even an exact trade, like carpentry for example, where you know why the table stands up or why it doesn't.

My question to people wanting to go full-time into counselling is not "Can you stand the responsibility?" but "Can you stand the ambiguity?" Does it matter to you that you may not be able to measure results, sometimes may not even be clear what the client came for in the first place?

What *is* clear, however, is that all clients have to have, to start with, a kind of relationship within which they can explore a problem and *find out* what else they need. And all the counsellor needs for that is genuineness, respect and empathy.

Getting the right words?

I have wandered somewhat from the starting point of the listening response illustrated, and have ended talking about a kind of relaxedness in the counsellor. There is another aspect of this comfortableness, which is not to become bound by the need to find the right words.

The last thing I want to do in illustrating the active listening/understanding type of response is to suggest there are special forms of words or "correct answers".

Every counsellor will develop his or her own style. In the case we are looking at, the counsellor might just as well have said (looking directly at the man):

"Three weeks, eh . . . ?"

and it would also have been a listening response. It would draw the client out further, would show the counsellor's attention and – the essence of listening at this early stage – would pick up from something the client himself said, inviting him to continue.

In his third response the counsellor in fact says nothing. One may imagine that the counsellor will continue to look towards the client, maybe look sympathetically at him, and the inviting silence says: "You haven't quite finished what you were saying".

There are a number of different ways of drawing out which were listed in Chapter 9. They all convey the same two things from the counsellor's side:

"I want to understand."

"Tell the story from your point of view."

Type 2 Response (probing)

"Right, then." [With a smile.] *"Let's start with a few facts, shall we?"* [Taking a pad] *". . . now you are –?"*

"Brian Lavery."

Commentary. Nothing wrong with this. The air of competence, friendliness and authority can be reassuring to the client. Yet it may be worth reviewing again the traps that asking too many questions can set for the counsellor.

Questions

First, it can put him in the position of the expert, in the client's eyes. Second, one question leads to another and this can turn into a steep and rather slippery slope for the counsellor.

"If I just answer all his questions", thinks the client to himself, "he'll be able to give me the solution." So he dutifully gives the answer and waits expectantly for the next question. And when the counsellor finally runs out of questions the client sits back even more expectantly and waits for the counsellor's considered opinion.

The counsellor, meanwhile, is wondering how to get out of the expert role he has landed in. The chances are that after a bit of throat-clearing there will be another question.

At this first stage the client needs to lead.

At the next stage, the counsellor may well need to probe, if only to fill out the bits of the picture the client seems to be avoiding. And later on still, the counsellor may *have* to be the expert. In a later phase – when, for example, they are trying to match the client's skills and experience with other job opportunities – the counsellor may well have to lead Brian through a structured series of questions to assess his relative strengths, interests, knowledge and abilities.

So one general rule about questions is: know why you are asking the question and what you are going to do with the answer. And it is not a bad idea either, if you need to embark on a particular series of questions, to tell the client *why* you are doing it that way.

Listening, then, at the first phase of counselling should not be confused with diagnosis. The client has to tell the story his own way and initially in his own time. Given the chance, clients are not all that bad at diagnosing themselves ("I do go round in circles, don't I?" "I've got this great big macho thing that the man has to be the breadwinner").

Listening is also more likely than questioning to carry the message to the client, right from the beginning: you and I are going to *share* the work, and the effort, and the energy that will go into solving this problem. A questioning approach right from the beginning may carry the implied message that as well as being in charge the counsellor is going to take major responsibility for finding the answers.

So there is another useful rule of thumb for counsellors: if they are doing more than 50 per cent of the work (putting in more than 50 per cent of the energy) to solve someone else's problem, they aren't doing counselling any more. They are probably doing what is called a "Rescue". And Rescuers have an uncanny habit of finishing up as Victims. ("Now look what you've made me do", says the client, "and you call yourself a counsellor!"). Or as Persecutors. ("Well, don't come here moaning every week, if you're not prepared to get off your backside and do something", says the counsellor. "I'm not going to keep on wasting my time, I can tell you that".)

The last trap in launching into an early round of questions is that it will bypass the emotional loading which the client needs to deal with. It may be OK when the doctor and the dentist fire their questions, because they need to, in order to find out what is wrong. And when the job is finished (the tooth is out or the bone is set) all the anxiety turns into relief and exhilaration. The emotional part is dealt with in the process of dealing with the physical. But counselling is not like dentistry.

Nor is much of medicine, for that matter. Any GP knows that sympathetic listening and enquiry will often do more than a prescription. Some GPs are now taking counsellors into their practice.

In counselling, the physical aspect usually plays a very small role. The emotional side is a central aspect of what the counsellor is directly dealing with. So it cannot usually be bypassed. Only when a counsellor knows of some procedure, has some vital information, has the real power to change a situation, can offer some immediate practical help, may he or she play more the role of the medic.

In those cases, of course, the counsellor should move straight into action. Nothing is likely to frustrate the client quicker than counsellors who continue to listen ("You really feel bad about it, don't you?"), when they could be *doing* something.

So much for the dangers of over-using the questioning mode. To be fair to beginner counsellors it is usually anxiety which prompts them to do it. The pressure to do or say something, anything; and the dreadful fear that they may run out of ideas.

Type 3 Response (interpreting)

"Ob, you're one of those people who like to take their time over things, are you!"

It may be said in friendly fashion, it does not perhaps have to be taken all that seriously. Yet already it carries the note that "I understand you as well as or better than you understand yourself". It carries the implication that the counsellor's job is to know about people. It somehow sets the counsellor apart. The counsellor is only called a counsellor because he or she knows something the client may not know.

It is an interpretative kind of response. It suggests that the counsellor has some general framework within which to slot people.

Again this does not mean that the counsellor *cannot* have some expertise. Only that this is not the time to bring it into play. Some people, even without formal qualifications in counselling, perhaps personnel people in organizations, have learned from sheer experience how to detect certain things – the signs of alcoholism, for example, or how depression manifests itself under various forms.

When starting to talk with someone, however, the counsellor will quietly file away such observations and concentrate on getting the story from the client as he or she describes it.

Type 4 Response (evaluating)

"Well, if it's three weeks, we need to get to grips with things as soon as possible. It's no use hanging about."

Once more, it is not a question of a poor response, only that it is mistimed at such an early stage. And it carries perhaps lightly the implication that the client has done something "wrong" in waiting so long. Even in such a slight sense it already implies that the counsellor sits in judgment, will say what is right and what is wrong. People can be quite sensitive to such nuances. At any rate, the response given is better than: "What the hell did you think we were here for, then?", which is also evaluative, and in my experience not inconceivable.

A counsellor will often see immediately in fact that the client is mistaken in some aspect of the problem, but challenging belongs to the *second* phase of counselling. Research shows very clearly that the first step in counselling is to establish a relationship within which the client feels free to talk openly. Any comment which indicates that the counsellor may take up a position *against* the client will at the very least slow down the building of that relationship.

It is a unique relationship in many ways, and when it is first offered the client may take some time to realize the freedom it offers, including the freedom to be *self*-critical. It is also a relationship within which the counsellor will have *earned* the freedom to challenge when the time is right.

Type 5 Response (supportive)

"Oh dear, oh dear. Let's see what we can do for you. Not the best thing in the world is it – though it may well be in the long run. Main thing is not to let it get you down."

Be honest now, how many of you would have picked this one as the most likely response? After "probing", the supportive response is the most popular and is usually offered in all sincerity and good will. Again, it is often not so much wrong as premature.

The supportive response is produced particularly by two kinds of counsellor: those who think that counselling is finding the shortest distance between problems and solutions; and those who rather wish (secretly? even without realizing it?) that problems could be solved without bringing feelings into the matter.

At its worst this kind of response says: "I'm afraid you've got the wrong feelings for this situation. You will need to change them if you are going to solve the problem."

Feelings

Nearly all counsellors have to learn to be more comfortable with feelings than they were when they first started. They may have to learn to simply sit with someone's feelings. They have to learn that, just because they are sitting with someone who is experiencing deep feelings, they are not automatically obliged to *DO* something.

Many of us spontaneously believe we have such an obligation because few of us will have escaped a kind of emotional "blackmail" at one time or other, which said (this is the common or garden variety) something like: "Now, see – you've upset mummy. Say you're sorry".

I am calling this emotional blackmail because it seems to put responsibility for one person's feelings on somebody else, and also to imply that it is only this second person who can make the first one's feelings better.

> It is the last part that counsellors are sometimes plagued by – the idea that if *they* don't do something to help the client's feelings, the client won't be getting what he needs. Hence the over-anxiety which prompts the counsellor to "take care of" the client's feelings ("Come on now, don't take on so!"; "Oh you poor thing"; "Not the end of the world, old sport!") before it's time.

Trying to do something about someone else's feelings as a first line of attack is almost always premature. Certainly at the beginning of counselling the client has to be allowed to *have* feelings before they are challenged in any way.

I hope it is clear that I am talking here about *counselling* situations. There are other situations of grief and hurt where people need comfort and *sympathy*, and where the emotional control which empathy demands is not enough.

Feelings in their natural form have a limited lifespan, in any case. Expressing them naturally will normally exhaust them. Interfering with this process is only likely to backfire.

Feelings tend to cloud clear thinking, but once feelings are vented people typically start thinking again. Trying to short-circuit directly into a client's thinking before the feeling has been properly expressed will usually only short-circuit into confusion, not clarity.

Later in the process, the counsellor may well have to challenge feelings directly. People get stuck in feelings; they nurse inappropriate ones; they manipulate others through their feelings; they refuse to give them up. It may well become part of the counsellor's job to prod someone out of a feeling – whether it be self-pity, revenge, timidity, jealousy or any other. But not at this stage.

The only thing clients need to know at this stage is that it is *safe* to have their feelings with this counsellor. And to express them.

Summary

The five categories of response (understanding, probing, interpreting, evaluating and supportive) carry different implications. Probing and supportive responses, in particular, may only serve to slow the counselling process down in its early stages.

PART II.   The Second Phase

Anyone who has engaged in counselling will have at least one story of a client who came in full of distress and complex problems, who then talked solidly for an hour and finally left, radiant and grateful, without having allowed the counsellor to say a word. Sometimes, however, such sympathetic listening is not enough. The feelings may have been cleared but the thinking has not. There still seems to be no way forward. Part II of *The Skills of Counselling* describes and illustrates the techniques a counsellor uses in the middle phase of the process.

Chapter 11   defines the essential characteristics of the second phase, its intuitive nature and its more challenging style.

Chapter 12   breaks down, with numerous examples, the different aspects of "advanced empathy" or second-level active listening, which is the core skill in this phase.

Chapter 13   isolates the other skills and techniques of Phase II, all related to empathy but all containing an element of challenge.

Chapter 14   sounds a note of caution about becoming too technical, or being too enthusiastic with one's confrontation.

Chapter 15   gives an extended example, with commentary, of an informal counselling session, illustrating typical aspects of Phase II techniques.

11   WHAT PHASE II DOES

The main task of Phase II is to *change the picture* for the client. He or she has to define the problem in a fresh way. The way the problem is stated up to now does not allow of a satisfactory conclusion. It needs to be stated in different terms.

Julie's husband is away a lot of the time and she herself is cramped in developing her career – she is a director with a public relations firm. The couple have three children under six. Ironically, her husband is engaged in important charitable work but he has little time at home.

Julie defines the problem as "He doesn't give me enough support with the children."

As long as she insists on that definition, there is only one range of options, all of them involving her *husband* doing something about it. But once the problem is defined as: "*I need more support with the children*", then new options are open to Julie, including looking elsewhere for support. It does not necessarily mean an extra-marital affair, maybe rather a broader base of support from friends, colleagues and baby-sitters. With the problem redefined, new choices open up.

This is a deliberately simple example to illustrate a point. Julie's story, as given, is only one facet of it. Of course she needs her husband's support for herself, too.

Another factor is that, until now, she has been refusing a live-in nanny because she has strong feelings about parents needing to be involved with growing children. At the same time she is rather proud of her husband's work and does not really want him to give it up. Typically, there are shifting feelings and conflicting values, all of which would need to be sorted, understood, reassessed.

Yet, however simplified the version may be, it highlights the fact that sometimes only a slight shift in the way a person thinks about a problem allows it to be solved. Sometimes, even, it is only a gap in awareness, something they had not fully realized.

Pauline is a chargehand in her fifties. She is a cheerful woman, very energetic and much liked. She is divorced and lives alone. She learned that she had breast cancer and that the chances of radiation or chemical treatments effecting a cure were poor. She was advised to have a mastectomy. She was naturally tremendously upset and her work and attitude slipped badly. Nobody knew what to do. Pauline was the sort of woman who helped everybody, but would never ask for help for herself. She tried to keep up a brave face.

Eventually Frances, one of the secretaries, asked her outright what was the matter and got the whole story. By chance, she herself had a friend who had gone through the same thing and passed on to Pauline something she had learned, which was that it is possible to have the breast reconstructed.

Pauline had never been told this, and it made all the difference to her. Why? Because what terrified her most was not the operation itself but the loss of her figure. One new fact made all the difference. The problem was not so much the cancer, but rather the loss of her femininity and her attractiveness to men, which still meant a lot to Pauline. The problem could now be managed, because with the new definition something could be done about it.

Again, a deliberately simple example. One might even say this is hardly counselling. It just so happened that a friendly colleague knew something Pauline did not. Maybe so, yet Frances also managed to do something which no one else had been able to do – get Pauline to talk.

However, the main point of the example is to illustrate a second feature of the middle phase of counselling. The client, as we have seen with Julie, needs to redefine the problem in order to move on. What the counsellor has to do is to *challenge* (provoke, prod, prompt, tease) her into doing it. And that means (totally unlike Phase I) that the counsellor has to add something, to contribute something, to change something in the client's picture.

Frances' contribution of sheer information is a simple case in point. She had won Pauline's trust. She clearly knew how to listen. And she happened to have some useful facts.

Usually, of course, things are more complicated. Yet the pattern is the same. It is the counsellor's contribution which makes the difference in Phase II – whereas in Phase I it was the counsellor's ability to understand. Maybe it will be only a matter of presenting a different perspective, as in the case of Julie. Maybe the client sees the glass as half-empty and needs to see it as half-full.

Changing a client's perception, then, is often the key to the door. There are other things which clients do, with or without malice aforethought, and which may have to be challenged, even forcefully confronted:

- [ ] they do not question their own motivation

- [ ] they do not realize that their own behaviour is betraying them

- [ ] they get stuck in some particular emotion (especially self-pity or resentment)

- [ ] they hang on to a bad feeling (sadness, for example) for far too long, to get people, or someone in particular, to react

- [ ] they say contradictory things

- [ ] they say things which simply are not true

- [ ] they are ignorant of quite elementary facts.

So Frances with her piece of information can stand as an example of how the counsellor's input is what turns the key in Phase II. As we shall see in Phase III, this input may increase dramatically.

What we can also see is that the contribution or input of the counsellor may or may not be welcome. The more challenging and confronting it is, the more delicate a task it becomes, and the clearer it is that the patient work of understanding in Phase I, letting the client see the non-judgmental nature of that understanding, building a sense of safety and trust – may all pay off now in Phase II.

The best counsellors still move cautiously. They sound rather hesitant as they search for a tactful way to do it.

Some writers say that good listeners acquire so much influence and credit with the client that they can afford to take risks in Phase II. This may be true, but it is usually wiser to move cautiously. It is still too easy to cash all one's hard-won credit by going straight in with hobnail boots. Usually, experience will teach the counsellor when to be more forthright.

If all the techniques of Phase II, however tentatively and carefully used, are essentially *challenging* skills, they may equally be said to have their origin (and their power) in a heightened understanding of the client. The textbooks call it *advanced empathy,* and I will be calling it *second-level active listening.*

More will be said about it in the next chapter. I will simply say here that the difference between empathy in Phase I and so-called advanced empathy is that in the first phase counsellors focus on the content of what is said, but in the second phase they may also reflect the *packaging* too. Not only what is said but *how* it is said; not only the facts but the more hidden feelings behind them; not just what is said but what is *not* said – what the person is not even aware of having said.

> *"You say you have put in a good performance this year, in fact you are full of it and I'm sure you are right; and yet you sound sad when you say it."*
>
> [Silence] *"Well I am sad that I'm only at the point now where I could have been three years ago if I hadn't taken time out to try to start a business."*

This ability to get at unexpressed feeling, at discrepancies and contradictions, and to bring them out is a major aspect of this second-level active listening.

Summary and conclusion

Phase II changes the picture in some significant way. Some new element makes it possible to see there is a way forward. If Phase I clears the feeling, Phase II clears the thinking. By the end of this second phase an objective or goal can safely be determined, leaving it to the last phase to find the means.

In this second phase (unlike the first) the counsellor's own contribution is critical. This contribution is essentially one of adding to, taking away from, changing, maybe even disputing the client's version of the picture. There is an element of challenge in most Phase II techniques, which is why they are best underpinned by a sensitive and intuitive kind of awareness of what the client is thinking and feeling – an ability I called second-level active listening.

As we move on to consider all this in detail, it may help to remember that "technique" ought not to make us too "technical". Counselling is a very personal activity, based on personal qualities like genuineness and an attitude of respect. Techniques are useful because they have been observed to be what good counsellors actually do.

They also help the learner to compare them with techniques which no-so-good counsellors use, such as incontrovertible logic, advice which cannot be faulted, immediate offers of help and some hearty cheering up.

It is usually rather easy to see where other people are going wrong, where they are not thinking straight, where they have got themselves emotionally confused. The temptation is to plunge in and straighten them out. But the emphasis of good counselling is always to let the clients find their own solutions and to challenge them sympathetically and tactfully.

12   SECOND-LEVEL LISTENING

In this chapter we explore the way in which counsellors develop their listening ability to a deeper level and single out some of the ways in which they communicate such sensitive understanding through:

☐ *picture-painting*

☐ *making the implicit explicit*

☐ *risking a hunch*

☐ *putting two and two together*

☐ *picking out themes*

☐ *drawing conclusions.*

■ ■ ■ ■

SECOND-LEVEL LISTENING

This is the big one. If active listening is the major skill of Phase I, advanced empathy or "second-level active listening" is the logical extension of it and the heart of Phase II. Again, it includes the ability to understand and to *communicate* understanding.

But in other ways it is radically different.

Where first-level empathy stays faithfully with the client and is essentially a *drawing-out* process, second-level empathy begins to bite, to challenge, even to jolt. If the non-judgmental understanding responses of the earlier stage acted like a poultice, the more penetrating understanding of the second stage is like a probe. At the first stage the client needs to learn the security and trust of having a shadow who seems able to understand and accept a messy picture and even to make better sense out of it than he had himself.

Now, suddenly the shadow swings out from behind, wheels in front of the client and looks him in the eye.

Susan is bemoaning the fact that she didn't get the new supervisor post.

"That's the second time. When Marian left last year I was living in hope. When they split the job just after Christmas and needed two people to supervise I was sure I'd get one of them. I mean what am I doing wrong? It's nine years now and I haven't missed a single day through illness. I just get on with the job, stay out of trouble, don't get involved – and what do I get? They ignore me. I sometimes wonder if they'd notice if I wasn't there. Perhaps I'd do better to be a loudmouth like Christine."

At the first stage the counsellor (Martin) would probably be more concerned to reflect and verify the different elements in the girl's remarks. He would include Susan's good work record, her relative quietness compared with the other girl, and the irritation and disappointment of being passed over in her favour.

The counsellor would add nothing. It may sound rather non-committal on paper, but with genuine interest and sympathy it would be just what Susan wants, to start with. She has not yet risked any real exploration of the matter and an understanding (listening) reply will simply prompt her to keep going.

"Well, that's right! I couldn't stand the woman from the day she first walked into the place. I don't like bossy women anyway, but they're the ones who seem to get the jobs."

However, if we presume that Susan has passed the point of getting it all out on the table and trusts Martin to be basically on her side, then he might try something more challenging.

"Strange how things turn out without you intending it. I mean there you go, always on your best behaviour, making yourself practically invisible, then all of a sudden they start looking straight through you when it comes to promotion. Don't even see you any more. Only see the showoffs. That's what's so aggravating."

Three things need to be said about this reply. First, it is empathetic, because it reflects something which Susan herself had partly implied – the idea of "invisibility" – through her words "ignore" and "notice".

Second, it adds from Martin's side the slightly new twist or slant that Susan had been playing a self-defeating role all along, that it is partly her own fault.

It is this which might shock or upset Susan. So Martin ought not to risk it till Susan is ready for it. It is a Phase II manoeuvre.

Third, Martin will therefore have to have his timing right, and if not sure, will have to be tentative. If his timing is off, Susan will probably read his comment as sarcastic and reply in kind:

> *"Thanks very much then. So it's all my own fault is it? Thank you very much. Glad I came to talk to you!"*

At some point, however, Martin has to get across the idea (which Susan had tried to keep out of sight, out of her own awareness) that she is her own worst enemy. When the time is right, that is the issue she has to face, not the other woman, Christine. She may have to become more assertive. She may not know there is a difference between being assertive and being brash.

TIMING, TENTATIVENESS AND CHALLENGE

So it is a matter of timing and, when not sure, being tentative. At some time the risk *must* be taken because Susan will only be helped for a limited time by being allowed to feel sorry for herself. It is only when she sees she has not been helping her own cause that she can start *doing* something about it. Timing in counselling, as in any sport or any art, is a matter of practice. Being careful and tentative about wading in with Phase II skills will save the counsellor from needless mistakes.

> In the long run the only real mistake would be *not* to risk confronting Susan. Some counsellors are too afraid to hurt. They wouldn't make good doctors and they don't make good counsellors. They are either afraid to hurt (on the mistaken grounds that the client "has already been hurt enough") or they are afraid to "intrude". So they never leave Phase I.

Phase II, then, is where the counsellor has to start getting tough. It can mean some strong medicine for the client. In this first example of advanced active listening the counsellor accurately picked up what Susan was saying, and threw the ball back.

Somebody once compared empathy with pairs skating, where one person leads and the other follows, like a mirror image.

But that is only first-level listening. At level two the second skater suddenly tests out a new movement of his own and momentarily jolts his partner. At level two, the mirror starts talking back on its own behalf, twisting the reflection in new ways to see if it still makes sense. There are a number of techniques for doing this.

Picture painting

One way is to use *images* and metaphors. The best counsellors are quite intuitive. They may not even know where an accurate intuition came from. But in fact it usually comes from some picture which floats across their mind. In the example of Martin and Susan, while Susan is talking about her bad luck, something she says creates the picture of The Invisible Woman, with everyone around her looking through her. It is this image which Martin feeds back to Susan, ("You've been trying to be The Invisible Woman and now it's gone too far – they've actually stopped seeing you".)

The main work of the middle phase of counselling, as has already been said, is "changing the picture" and this ability to paint a picture for the client is perhaps the single most valuable skill a counsellor can have at this point.

It is not as rare as it may sound. It may seem that level one listening was hard enough and that level two listening must be even more intense. This is not the case. In many respects level two listening is more relaxed. One is not struggling to pick up all the detail and to remember the different strands. Rather, one is focusing in a relaxed way on the general drift, asking oneself: "What is the client saying generally, in one sentence?", or, better still, "in one *picture?*"

This is the essence of what has been called listening with the third ear. It actually does not require as much sheer effort as listening with the other two. Nor does it require unusual mental ability. Some quite ordinary people, not even particularly verbal, can create and paint word pictures better than they can produce long paragraphs.

If this particular listening skill is rare, it is not so much because it is difficult but because a counsellor has to learn to relax, and to relax will usually mean having had enough experience to be more open and to be less concerned about making a mistake. This is all simply a matter of time – and supervision, if that is available.

We may perhaps remind ourselves too that listening in the context of counselling means being able to *hear* accurately what another person is saying and to *feed it back* accurately. It is not just the ability to keep silent but an ability to communicate. Again, it is not a passive skill but a highly active one.

> If the communication at Phase I is to accurately reflect what one has heard, the communication in Phase II is to tentatively suggest what one *may* have heard.

It is not only an active skill, but it is the source of great influence over a client. It is a skill which can be developed and sharpened like any other. It can be immensely useful in a range of other situations apart from counselling.

There are a number of ways in which this level two listening skill is shown, where a kind of relaxed concentration will take the client further than the simple reflecting techniques of Phase I. We have looked at *picture-painting* as one of them. Here are some others.

Making explicit what is only implicit

Martin and Susan are a good example of this. When Martin brings out that Susan has been trying to *make* herself invisible he has brought something out which was only half said by Susan. Indeed Susan may not even have been aware of it. In an earlier example, when the counsellor says: "Your words are enthusiastic yet you look sad", he is bringing something out which was conveyed, yet not deliberately.

 "It drives me mad! If only she'd talk! Yet the minute I say something she flares up and we're back into an argument."
   "Does that mean that she sees you as the one who starts the fight?"
"Well, I never thought of that. It certainly wasn't my intention." [He looks startled.]

The counsellor has jolted the client by bringing a new element into the picture which was in shadow before but is now suddenly highlighted. Without being accusing he has prompted the client into thinking about things in a different light.

This particular example comes close to another type of Phase II challenge, which is *risking a hunch*. It can be a dangerous game because it can tempt the counsellor into some pretty wild guesswork. It always runs the risk that the guess is really a projection and that means it is part of the counsellor's thinking, not the client's. It may also run the counsellor close to interpretation, which is a skill that needs careful monitoring and checking and is best left to the professionals.

Yet a hunch can always be checked. It is a kind of intuitive probing, and is another skill which can be sharpened. Some people are naturally quite intuitive and if the intuition is presented carefully and gently and the counsellor is quick to withdraw if it is off the mark, then a hunch may make a sudden breakthrough which pushes the client quickly to a new understanding of the problem.

"You know, every time you have one of these anxiety attacks it seems to come shortly after one of your famous 'project meetings'. Is there any connection do you think?"

"Really? I suppose that's true, though I hadn't noticed it. I wonder . . . ?"

Again, the skills of the middle stage of counselling often overlap. This last example illustrates another typical counselling skill of this phase, that of . . .

Putting two and two together

"You come to talk to me because of your drinking problem, and yet you are now talking the whole time about the way your two teenagers are playing up. Are they trying to tell you something about your drinking, do you think?"

Another aspect of the same skill is *picking out themes* or threads.

"I've been going through in my mind all the various things we have been talking about and the one which seems to link them all together is how often you say this or that 'makes you feel bad'. It seems as though almost anything can make you feel guilty, even when you are clearly in the right. I know for a fact you were right about the last incident, yet you still imagine you must be at fault. Maybe you need to start thinking differently about things – and about yourself?"

Here again there is an overlap. This last example might also be classified as a confrontation. It brings the client up short with a direct challenge to a characteristic way of thinking. Yet again it shows that confrontation does not have to be a negative manoeuvre. It may even be kindly.

Drawing conclusions

"I know you haven't said it but if you can't stand the man and if you have decided there is nothing to be gained by complaining, the logical alternative would be to quit and look elsewhere. Is that logical or are you not even willing to think about it?"

Again, different elements of Phase II skills are interwoven. As well as drawing conclusions this might just as easily be thought of as making something explicit which was only implicit. It might also be considered a confrontation.

Summary

All of Phase II revolves round two basic skills: advanced empathy (second-level active listening) and a challenge in the way one puts one's comments. Phase I was about accuracy, understanding and acceptance. Like a poultice which continually "draws out" more and more. Phase II is less like a poultice; rather, it acts as a probe. Like other kinds of probe, the more sensitively and the more economically it is used the better. I have examined some of the techniques for doing this.

13   OTHER SKILLS OF PHASE II

Second-level active listening is the central element in Phase II of counselling.
The counsellor's responses, as well as being empathetic, are at this stage also
likely to be penetrating. Some of the things good counsellors do at this stage –
things which may challenge or surprise or stimulate the client into thinking
again – include:

☐ *summarizing*

☐ *giving information*

☐ *confronting*

☐ *talking about one's own experience*

☐ *immediacy*

☐ *probing*

☐ *encouraging.*

■ ■ ■ ■

SUMMARIZING

Counselling sometimes means keeping two or three things in mind at once.
The most usual thing for a "new" counsellor is to hang on to one thing, to go
chasing down the one avenue which seems the most interesting or
important. What is important or interesting for the counsellor, of course,
may not be so for the client.

So what counsellors have to do is to mentally note two or three aspects of
what is being said. Then when they have filled up their short-term memory
bank they need to check with the client if they are up to date. ("Have I
understood correctly?")

We first looked at the skill of summarizing at Phase I. There it is relatively
passive. It is imbued with the simple idea that the counsellor is concerned to
understand sincerely and without comment how the problem looks to the
client.

In Phase II, summarizing plays a different role. Here it is usually a bridging
skill *between* Phase I and Phase II.

By this time the whole story is out and the client has satisfied himself that the counsellor is now in possession of all the facts. He has come to the point where he is clearer and calmer about what the core of the problem is. The summary at this point begins as a *resumé* of where the pair of them, counsellor and client, have got to.

At this point the counsellor is inviting the client to move into Phase II. The question now is not just "Have I understood how the problem looks and feels to you?", but "Have we now got all the elements in play?", and "Are they in the right perspective?"

If the summary is good and reflects accurately the thinkling and feeling which the client has expressed, he will pick up the summary and move forward.

It is clear that this kind of summarizing is not the relatively simple reflecting skill of Phase I. It requires a kind of sifting, a boiling down into a set of central points. It requires more than a listing, rather a *shaping* of the points made or even a *reshaping*.

> The way the summary is shaped marks the counsellor's first real contribution, because it can be shaped in a way which highlights certain aspects at the expense of others, and begins the typical process of Phase II which says "I understand the way you see the problem, but maybe there is another way". The client is being challenged, not just understood.

This is where the counsellor begins for the first time to do something *different*. Just putting the pieces together like this may be something the client has not been able to do for himself.

More than that, the counsellor's accurate summary may well include some aspect of the problem that the client has conveniently been choosing to "forget". When the summary shows that this aspect is still in play the client is obliged to face it afresh. "Yes, I suppose that's true. I still haven't really given up the idea of putting the house on the market. Perhaps I need to settle that bit once and for all."

It is in this way that the key element of Phase II is already introduced – challenge. If Phase I has been dealt with sympathetically and without judgment, the client can now feel that the challenge is given without malice or aggression. He is faced with something he had barely admitted to himself.

Now he is being pushed by the counsellor to continue to face himself with the truth.

But he faces it *with* the counsellor, not against him. The problem may still appear mountainous, but now the client has an ally. To one person at least the problem is seen in its true light, it is accepted in its hard reality, yet without criticism. Perhaps there is a way forward. Perhaps the counsellor has seen such situations before. Perhaps there is a solution. Perhaps there is a different way of looking at the hole thing.

It is in this sense that summarizing is a bridge between the first and second phases of counselling and also a challenge.

> *"Yes, it's the bonus scheme. I'd forgotten about that. It's too complicated. If we could sort that out a lot of other things would fall into place."*

So a point has been brought back into focus which the client would really rather forget, and is perhaps secretly hoping the counsellor will forget too because that is the one thing he or she finds it hard to face.

 Brian had talked at length about his bitterness over the redundancy notice and what he saw as unfair terms. He had talked about his limited chances of finding new work quickly, about retraining, about finance. He had also said how guilty it made him feel in front of his family and asked the counsellor if he thought it a good idea to keep on leaving the house every morning as usual, so no one would know what had happened. Then he had gone rapidly to other things.

But in his summary the counsellor had included the sentence: "Then there is the problem of telling or not telling your family." There was a long pause and then Brian sighed and said: "I really have to, don't I, I don't see how I could live a lie like that, or even get on with doing what I have to. I'm sure Beth would understand. In fact she would probably know best how to break it to the kids . . . no holidays this year and all that . . ."

Another pause, then:

"That's the only place to start really. I don't know how I'm going to do it but I'd better do it quickly. My God, it's awful. I have to get it over with. As soon as I can get her on her own

this evening. It's probably the worst thing I've ever had to
face. But it's not going to be much use talking to you until
I've brought her into it."

ADVICE GIVING

Some counsellors feel pressed to give advice when people come to them
with a problem. Brian even asked for the advice and probably the best
advice would be to tell his wife. But this counsellor-colleague was wise
enough to hold back and in the end Brian gave himself the best advice. He is
likely to be more committed if it is his own idea, and to that extent he can
also have the satisfaction of knowing it was his own solution which worked,
not someone else's.

This is the main reason for being cautious with advice; people will in the end
best follow advice they give to themselves and better keep their self-respect
in the process. Unfortunately some counsellors seem to think they have not
done a day's work if they have not handed out some advice. They do not see
that the skill of *enabling* the other person to make up his mind is equally
valuable.

There is also the problem that the most obvious advice is often
the very thing the client strenuously refuses to contemplate and
the counsellor will promptly lose credibility and may alienate the
client. There is also the occasional danger of the client who has a
habit of collecting advice, making a mess of it, then saying: "See
what you made me do!"

Of course, a counsellor should not simply be awkward about giving advice
if pressed. In Brian's case the counsellor could have said:

> *"I think if I had to face it myself I would have to tell my
> family – but that's me, not you. On the other hand I can
> also tell you I know this problem of telling the wife is often
> the worst sticking point for a lot of men. Yet much more
> often than not they come back and say – thank God I did."*

A significant aspect of what this counsellor says is that it also contains
information. Two pieces of information in fact: the likely results of doing a
particular thing; and the buried information that other people had to face
the same problem and had the same reaction to it. So it is not simply advice.

This is often the greatest relief to a client, especially where feelings are involved. It often happens that a person is faced with a difficult situation *and* on top of that with conflicting feelings about it. They may know other people have had to face the same situation but they do not know that their feelings about it are equally typical. It would be a relief to Brian to know that his shame was not something peculiar, but that a lot of other men felt it too.

Giving information

> *"It's true that a lot of people find the new paperwork more detailed than the old. Did you know that it is being done that way to comply with EEC regulations on export documentation which come into force at the beginning of the year?"* [And the person says:] *"Oh, I see – no, nobody told us that. We all thought it was that crazy new admin manager with his new-fangled ideas."*

Information-giving is one of the more obvious skills in the middle phase of counselling. We have already given an example in the case of Pauline and Frances at the beginning of the chapter, and another from Brian's counsellor. An experienced manager I know says he is amazed how often it is a lack of information which is the source of a problem for his "clients".

Occasionally, however, it is not obvious that lack of information is the root of a problem. A good indication that this may be the case is when the problem does not seem to make any sense, when the counsellor does not see *how* something can be a problem. It usually happens when the *client* is not aware of some fact which the counsellor takes for granted and imagines that everyone knows. A counsellor should never be afraid to appear dim-witted, so the obvious question is: "Sorry, I don't understand. *How* is this a problem for you?"

Confronting

> *"You say you never get any credit for your part in the team's success, yet ten minutes ago you were delighted with the extra commission you all shared. There must be something else bugging you apart from the money."*

Challenge or confrontation is meat and drink to many a would-be counsellor, but in fact it is only one technique among many and is usually most effective when it points to a discrepancy in what people say, when this is documented by facts and behaviour, when it is inescapable and when it is softened by some sort of compassion.

It is worth emphasizing that confrontation comes best from what has been called "a caring position". It can be hard without being hurtful.

One client recounting his experience with a counsellor said: "I told him the others all thought I was weird – and do you know what he said? He said, 'Well, you are weird!'" Obviously, the comment had been made in a way which showed it was not a condemnation. In some odd way it was even reassuring. The man could be "weird", but that did not mean he was unacceptable to the counsellor. A statement and a confrontation like that can often be delivered best with a laugh.

> It doesn't come through in a lot of texts on counselling and psychotherapy, and it may not come through in this one, but humour is one of the greatest assets of a counsellor. It can break a logjam, it can defuse tension, it can make a fairly rough confrontation palatable. It can be a safeguard for the counsellor, too. It takes a while for some counsellors to drop the solemnity with which they treat every revelation of the client. One of the most helpful comments I ever had from my own supervisors was that I tended to take clients too seriously.

As well as being a separate technique in itself, confrontation or challenge is one of the two underlying techniques in the whole of Phase II. There is a further word of caution about it in Chapter 14.

Talking about one's own experience

This may be too easy a temptation for the beginner, but it has its place.

> *"You know, there never was any sort of incentive scheme in this company until three years ago and I often feel a bit resentful that I was too late to qualify."*

It only works when the revelation is genuinely personal, when it matches the level at which the person has revealed him or herself. The effect has to be that the client is startled into thinking "I'm not unique. Other people have been hurt in the same way." What does not work is a superficial or phoney revelation which effectively discounts the person:

> *"Young man, when I was your age we didn't even know the meaning of incentive schemes."*

To quote another experienced manager:

> *"Talking about oneself, in my view, is an almost universal fault among the untrained or unthinking. You need to put more stress on the dangers of doing this."*

Immediacy

This is the term researchers have coined for those occasions when the counsellor needs to talk about the way the relationship is developing between the counsellor and the client.

> *"We seem to be back at the same old starting-point. I get the feeling we are going round in circles. Whenever I bring up the matter of the way you relate to other departments you sort of yawn as though you think I'm off course. I feel you are simply refusing to talk about it, that you are telling me to back off, yet you don't actually say so. Am I right?"*

Probing

> *"You keep saying you are no good. Give me some examples."*

> *"What do you mean, you 'keep going over the top'. What does that mean?"*

The counsellor may need to push the client to be specific. Clients sometimes try to get away with vague or general statements and they may have to be pushed into being clear what they mean, or the counsellor will never get to the bottom of the generally self-defeating picture they paint and so will never be able to change it.

Encouraging

> *"You talk about getting the necessary experience in three years. But the way you go about things and the energy you put into it you could easily finish in two."*

That is *changing the picture* in an encouraging way, not merely encouragement for the sake of it. To say only: "Come on, you always look on the dark side of things", may be encouraging, but sometimes it will sound like telling the person not to *feel* a certain way.

These last two categories (probing and encouragement or support) are two that were excluded when we discussed Phase I skills. But they have their place here, in Phase II. Encouragement and support may well play a part in Phase III too.

Summary

In this chapter we have looked at a series of specific techniques to move a client through the logjam of a problem which even when understood and summarized at the end of Phase I still seemed insoluble. All these techniques contain an element of challenge and all are underpinned by the sensitive understanding and communication of second-level listening.

There are variations to these approaches, but the principal thrust of all of them, of the whole of Phase II, is that they are intended to move the client to think differently about his or her problem, to put it into a new framework, to shuffle the pieces of the puzzle in such a way that a goal, a way forward or some action can emerge at the end.

Action will be the work of Phase III, and Phase III may include advice-giving, which I have temporarily excluded as a technique of Phase II. I have given a number of reasons why a counsellor should not be too quickly inveigled into offering advice. In Chapter 15 I show again how the question of giving advice can be handled. Meantime, I need to stand back from technique for a moment or we will not see the wood for the trees.

14   CAUTIONS

Because of their importance, two aspects of the counselling process are briefly extracted again in this chapter, in order to reinforce them.

■ ■ ■ ■

DON'T BE TOO TECHNICAL

There is always a danger with a breakdown such as the list of separate techniques I elaborated in the last chapter that what is simple suddenly looks too technical. When an art critic dissects a Michelangelo painting it can take all the artistry, not to mention the pleasure out of it. And there is no doubt that counselling is an art and a tremendous satisfaction.

So let us remind ourselves that what makes counselling-helping effective is the *PERSON* of the counsellor and not the method. There is no such thing as counselling-by-numbers. If the person helping has learned to respect other people's views, can be simple and straightforward without putting on a pose and has the ability to put himself in the other person's shoes, then that is all that is needed. To be oneself may lead to "technical" blunders. But it is more important in counselling to be oneself than to be faultless. What counts is the sensitivity and humility to acknowledge mistakes and to recoup. It counts for far more than the artificiality and stiltedness which a preoccupation with mistakes and technique will induce.

If there is an additional quality required for Phase II it is that the counsellor needs to have the *courage* to challenge the client when the time is right. If the central point of Phase I is *LISTENING*, the central aspect of Phase II is *CONFRONTING* empathetically.

CONFRONTATION

Confrontation in the counselling process is a gentler procedure than is usually implied in general usage. It *may* mean eyeball to eyeball but this is not of the essence.

The point is that, like everyone else, clients can delude themselves. Not only may they not be thinking straight, they may also not be fully honest with themselves; may stubbornly refuse to see something; decide something; change something; do something. Then the problem can never be tackled until they are tackled personally. They have to be challenged to give up something – a mistaken belief (however cherished); a feeling; mental blinkers; wilful ignorance; an entrenched attitude.

In the first phase, the counsellor will let such things go, will make no comment. In the second phase he or she has to take a risk in issuing a challenge. If willingness to make mistakes is part of the counsellor's make-up, so is willingness to take risks. As a matter of fact, the simple drawing-out techniques of Phase I will often do the trick themselves:

> *"You mean the marketing man has refused outright to have anything to do with it?"*

> *"Well, um, not exactly outright."*

> *"But when you asked him he made it quite clear."*

> *"Well, I didn't exactly ask him directly . . ."* [Falls silent.]

But in Phase II the confrontation may have to be more direct:

> *"I've talked to the marketing man, you know, and he says you never actually asked him."*

So it may be useful to suggest one or two general "rules" about confronting.

The rules of confrontation

☐ 1. The helper needs to have *earned the right* to confront the other person. He or she needs to have put some thought and effort into producing the kind of safe atmosphere where confrontation can be accepted and used. The other rules all follow from this.

☐ 2. It will be done carefully, which means with care in both senses of the word: with care and with caring.

☐ 3. It will be done tentatively. The challenge of Phase II is like tapping on a pane of glass to produce the tiniest hairline cracks. Only rarely will it mean the sharp decisive crack which is intended to split the glass in a particular way.

☐ 4. The helper will be very clear that the confrontation does not come directly from his own frustration and exasperation, to serve the primary purpose of relieving his own feelings. It may well do that, because people can be exasperating, but it can still be timed so that it is the *client's* needs which are chiefly in view.

☐ 5. The helper leaves himself open to be confronted in turn. The relationship of counselling is not a one-way street.

☐ 6. Let clients challenge or confront themselves whenever possible.

And so on. There are doubtless other "rules" of successful confrontation. This sample is meant to give a flavour to a delicate (and very satisfying) part of the counselling process.

Conclusion

It may be interesting to come back to the whole of this middle section of the book after a few weeks of practice and look at it again. It is not intended to say: This is how you must do it. Anyone who takes it in that sense will lose spontaneity and freedom as a person.

But the examples are worth reviewing from time to time, because they are illustrations of what good counsellors have been observed to do in practice. They represent a range of skills which can be acquired step by step in the same way that today's masters did when they were yesterday's apprentices.

15   PHASE II EXAMPLE – CONNIE

As an additional example at the end of Phase I it was more useful to illustrate a whole range of separate and different responses. Here, to illustrate Phase II, we need more of a continuous conversation. This one took place on the 'phone. You do not need an office, an appointments diary and a certificate on the wall to do counselling – although it must be admitted that in this case Pam, the friend, had had some training.

■ ■ ■ ■

That was not why Connie called her. Or was it? Connie said she saw Pam as someone who could be objective and someone who would not just give her answers she thought would please her. As good a tribute as any professional could wish for.

The situation is on the boundary between Phase II and Phase III. Connie has to make a decision over the weekend and take action on Monday morning. The counsellor is not going to be rushed, however. She listens a little, in a quiet, Phase I fashion; does rather more at Phase II, using different techniques; and in less than 15 minutes Connie is thinking clearly again. She does not need anything at Phase III. She knows what she has to do and needs no help in carrying it out.

Moving out of Phase I . . .

> *"Pam, I can't make my mind up. I applied for this part-time nursing post at the local hospital, which is better than the crummy job I've got now. Anyway they offered it to me and I turned them down – but now I don't know what to do."*

> *"Hold on! Let me get that straight. You applied for a job, you got it, but you changed your mind. Now you are wondering about changing it back again? You mean going back to the hospital and saying yes?*

A typical Phase I response, checking understanding. It shows interest and the wish to understand, and draws Connie out further with its hanging question-mark.

"That's right! Well, it turned out a bit different from what they said it was. I mean I would be on nights three months of the year at least, plus some weekends. And with Eddie away more and more, the domestic side could get pretty chaotic . . . "

"Yes . . . sounds like a lot of overload for both of you."

A simple Phase I "reflecting" response. There is no particular merit in the actual words used. It could have been said in half a dozen different ways. What Pam manages to convey is that she is trying to imagine how it must be for Connie, including how it must *feel*. Hence she tries "overload" to see if that reflects back closely enough. And includes "both of you" to see if Connie mentioned her husband for some particular reason – as it turns out, apparently not.

"That's right [sigh] *. . . it just seems an awful lot of hassle.* [Pause] *And is that what we need right now? OK I know Tim's sixteen, but it's his GCSE year . . . "*

The counsellor could have made another reflective comment here or made a first brief summary. But Connie is apparently thinking aloud and there is no real need to interrupt her. Silence used like this can be companionable rather than awkward. Either way, silence is a great drawing out technique. Full marks to the counsellor for knowing how to keep her mouth shut.

. . . And into Phase II

"To be honest I didn't really expect to get the job after all this time away from regular nursing. They even said they'd take me on the relief squad if I didn't want the part-time job –"

"Well done! They really want you!"

"Yes – and Mr Cunningham (that's the boss on the morning job) said it would be alright for me to be called out in an emergency, provided I made the time up somehow. Anyway, I finally said no to the nursing job and now I'm kicking myself. You know how I get. There's still time to go in on Monday morning and tell them I've changed my mind. They said they would leave it open till then. But you know how I am with decisions these days. Never sure if it's the right one. What do you think I should do?"

"I'll tell you what I think – not too sure about the 'should' bit. And yes, I DO know how you go backwards and forwards on decisions. But let me check a couple of things first. What other pressures are there on you, swaying you this way or that?"

A quick bit of footwork. Pam neatly ducks out of advice-giving at such an early point. In most cases clients do not want advice even when they ask for it. Sometimes, of course, they do and they welcome it. You can always test by *giving* the advice. If the first words out of the client's mouth are "Yes, but", you will know it is not advice they want; possibly information, more probably support, conceivably a fight. Anyway, advice for the counsellor is like price for a salesman – he wants to talk about everything else first.

So Pam postpones the advice, makes an echoing statement to let Connie know she has registered the bit about going round in circles and moves into *PROBING*.

This is Phase II questioning. It goes beyond the "Tell me what *you* need, to get me to understand" invitation of Phase I. The implication is more: "This is what *I* need to know, to be able to help you"; or "This is what you *must* think about to solve your problem". That is why it is more of a probe than a poultice. It may touch some soft spots. Questions at Phase II are often a challenge to the client. All the more reason why they should not be aggressively put. This is a good open question.

"What do you mean?"

"I mean Eddie, about the money angle – about anything connected with the job."

"Oh well, Eddie isn't pushing me one way or the other. He's leaving the decision to me. I know it must suit him better to have me at home nights and weekends. Suits me better too. Anyway, he agreed pretty quickly when I said I'd decided not to take the hospital job. But that's part of the trouble. I get the impression everyone is agreeing with me. I don't know if they mean it or they're saying it to please me, or if it's just because it suits them. That's why I want your opinion. You're usually pretty rational and objective."

"Yes, I can see that. It's a bit like shouting in the hills – all you get back is an echo. OK, I'll see if I can do better than that. So what about the money?"

"Oh yes. Well it doesn't make much difference really. The job I have now doesn't pay anywhere near as much as nursing. But it gives me more hours, so in fact I'd be slightly better off as I am."

"But money isn't the deciding factor?"

"No, not at all."

"One last thing . . . if you went over to nursing and it didn't work out, could you come back to the job you have now?"

"Not a chance. Nobody is being asked to leave, but they are shedding labour at every opportunity they can get. You know, when people leave of their own accord, I mean."

"Alright, you asked me what I thought. The first thing I think is that you have thought about it pretty logically yourself. Anything I can think of, you've already worked out yourself and taken it into account. So you arrive at a perfectly good decision to turn down the hospital job, and THEN you start hassling yourself."

So Pam tells Connie what she thinks. Quite right. She has listened and now it is time to talk. This would be the wrong time to continue with Phase I listening skills – "You want to know what I think. Tell me more about that". That would be enough to make the client scream. So Pam talks. She will need to be alert for "Yes, buts" and go back to listening if she gets them.

In fact Connie responds positively and Pam goes straight into an advanced empathy technique – what I have been calling second-level listening – which requires some imaginative, sensitive, tentative, half-humorous exploring of what lies *behind* the obvious content.

In this case it is the conflicting internal dialogue in Connie's mind.

"Don't I just!"

"Sounds like you start talking to yourself. Or some weird voice in your head does . . . what does it say!"

"Oh, something like: 'Why don't you get something worthwhile instead of a job any moron could do.'"

"'We didn't put you through nursing school for nothing, you know'".

"Exactly!"

"'We had to make quite a few sacrifices didn't we?'"

"Stop it! It's bad enough without you doing it too!"

"And what did the voice say when you decided to go for the hospital job?"

"Oh, then it said: 'There you go thinking about yourself. It's the kids who'll have to pay for it. And Eddie too . . . There's another five years yet before you need to be thinking about a full-time career'".

"H'm, well you asked me what I thought. I already said you seem to have thought the thing through pretty well yourself. Now I can't do anything about the voices telling you contradictory things, but logic says that if you are going to clobber yourself whatever you decide, then at least choose the thing YOU most want. And every time you talk about the hospital job and the weekends and the nights you sigh like a crazy woman. You ask me what you SHOULD DO, but you have enough voices tell you that. You've also been saying clearly enough what you WANT to do, which is keep the present job, however crummy it's supposed to be. I can't see any good reason why you shouldn't, if you want me to be objective. There's one other thing, but it's more about me than you. What do you think?"

So Pam gives her advice. She also feeds back the non-verbal part of what Connie has been saying, the packaging, namely her sighing. She then goes to another Phase II technique – talking about oneself. She is careful to advertise it as such and asks if Connie wants it.

"Yes, of course. Say it."

"It's this. When I get stuck in a decision myself, I tend to make one I can go back on most easily. Or I make half a change rather than a complete change. In this case, if you switch over to the nursing job you can't go back. On the other hand you do have the option of going onto the hospital relief roster. And once you are there, you will be closer to other openings that may appear. And the hospital people will be getting to know you. I know your youngest is still only eleven. You may want to wait before you get back into full-time hospital or nursing work. With the relief squad experience you'll be keeping in touch and you'll be

more aware of other opportunities that open up. Seems to make sense. What do you think?"

"It's true. You are logical, you know! OK – I've made the decision already. I'll leave it where it is."

"There is another thing, Connie. Yes?"

"Yes?"

"Those voices are still a pest for you. If you ever want to try and nail them, once and for all, give me a buzz and we'll meet somewhere. It's not really something for a phone call like this . . ."

"OK, I will. It's something that gets me down in all sorts of ways. Thanks . . ."

Pam contents herself with reinforcing Connie's clear thinking. There is no doubt that she uses her influence in a straightforward way (a Phase III skill). And she offers more help if wanted.

A good example of how to end a counselling session. There is always more to be done. It is a great temptation for the counsellor to try and remake the client in one interview.

PART III. The Third Phase

The third stage of the counselling process is about two things: on the client's side *ACTION*, and on the counsellor's side assisting and *RESOURCING* that action. The main characteristic of the third phase, compared with the previous two, is already clear. It requires much more from the counsellor in terms of *service* and practical help. Phases I and II may be sufficent in many cases, but there are others where they are not. Particularly in the work situation, counselling may be linked with performance and with a positive outcome; and there may not be all the time in the world. The general philosophy of counselling may insist that the individual keeps final responsibility for solving the problem, but the counsellor still has a job to do. The third and last part of *The Skills of Counselling* describes how the counselling process may need to be completed and how it often issues into other forms of helping.

Chapter 16 shows the *link* between the third phase of counselling and the previous two, and also how its style is quite different.

Chapter 17 reviews the most important *types* of contribution the counsellor makes at this stage of the process.

Chapter 18 takes *career counselling* as one example of the "expert" or specialist aspect of Phase III.

16   COMPLETING THE PROCESS

For those who have a predilection for action the role of the counsellor in the last phase of the process will be more familiar territory. If they have been patient till now they will learn with relief that they can at last do something. If it is any further consolation, the chances are good that their contribution will now be all the more effective, more economical in terms of effort, and less prone to setbacks.

When we come to look at the sorts of thing a counsellor may do at this point of the process, we soon find ourselves constructing a long list, since there is almost any number of things clients may want us to do which they are genuinely unable to do for themselves. The counsellor will still have to decide what is appropriate for him or her to do and what is not.

The chapter is structured round three typical examples of Phase III work:

☐ *a simple service*

☐ *a coaching sequence*

☐ *a referral.*

These examples illustrate the different nature of Phase III counselling, and at the same time how it is an integral part of the whole process.

■ ■ ■ ■

Derek is the sales engineer we met in Chapter 1. He had been called "abrasive" by two customers and had become moody and difficult in the office. Given that this was a sharp change from his typical behaviour of the last seven years, his manager called him in, told Derek in a straightforward way what he had observed and had been told – and asked if there was something wrong or if there was something he himself could help with.

The story came out hesitantly at first because Derek was somewhat embarrassed, but faced with the genuine interest of the boss and his sympathetic drawing out of the facts, he finally said with a grimace that he was under financial pressure. His wife had gone into business for herself as an interior decorator but had lost money when two of her early creditors went bust. She had just picked up a new, high-volume contract but it would be some months before she started getting anything back.

Meanwhile, on the strength of last year's considerable joint earnings, they had invested in an old property and spent heavily renovating it. Derek was incidentally, and somewhat irrationally, resentful that his colleagues had at that time enjoyed his lavish hospitality but were now giving him nothing in return – though what they could do in practice he wasn't very clear.

The manager might have suggested Derek approach a professional debt counsellor. Such services exist and can cost very little. It was an option, but as it happened the manager was unaware of it. He did know, however, that his superiors were normally sympathetic to such situations and he was able to put his authority behind a request for an interest-free loan from the company, for the few months that Derek's wife needed to regain her income and stabilize their cashflow. A much relieved Derek was able to return his energy and interest to the job.

COUNSELLING AND HELPING

This book could have been called a guide to "counselling" *and* "helping". It would have made the point that the two are not entirely the same. All counselling is intended to be helpful, but not all helping is counselling. You can help me across the road without counselling me at all.

Some people say that what I am calling the third phase of the counselling process should not be called counselling at all but simple "helping". I have no quarrel with this. My point is that such helping is the natural continuation of counselling, as it was in the case of Derek. In many cases too the helping phase may never get off the ground if it is not underpinned by the counselling skills of the first two.

There is a danger in making too sharp a distinction between counselling and helping. It might distract the more concrete-minded counsellor from the fact that the first two phases can be extremely helpful – and more than that, may be the only help the client really wants. Any experienced counsellor will be able to recall a case where he or she was just geared up to move into Phase III when the client said: "Thanks very much – I prefer to do the rest myself."

The opposite situation also arises when the counsellor tries to put an abrupt end to proceedings at the end of Phase II and pushes the client out of the door with: "Sorry, I can't help you any more – I'm only a counsellor." This is not a fanciful example. Some excellent counsellors at Phases I and II are actually uncomfortable with the different demands of Phase III and prefer to bow out. They rationalize this phase as something totally other, called advice-giving or social work or consultancy, which they want no part of. But why not? If this is a part of what the person genuinely needs, is it not client-oriented to move with them?

COUNSELLOR AND CLIENT PREFERENCES

A counsellor needs to be aware of personal preferences for the different kinds of work involved in the three phases. The timid listener who is too afraid to hurt anyone and so never speaks his mind, the expert in newly discovered challenging techniques, and the "let's-get-on-with-it" brigade who propel you across the street without troubling to enquire why you are standing there – all are images (albeit overdrawn) of counsellors who have a strong preference for one or other of the three phases. They stand as a reminder that the complete counsellor will have some skills in all of them.

Clients too have preferences – those who welcome the warm cocooning of the first phase and are reluctant to emerge from it, those who relish the cut-and-thrust of the middle phase but are not really interested in doing anything, and those who come to the counsellor because "you are some kind of expert, aren't you?" and who expect to be told what to do and perhaps to have it done for them.

It goes without saying that these conflicting perceptions on both sides about what counselling involves may need to be brought into the open as part of the process itself. It is to pre-empt such conflicting notions that most modern texts put so much emphasis on the understanding or *contract* which counsellors make with clients at the very beginning.

ILLUSTRATION OF PHASE III WORK

Throughout the book there are examples of the typical situation where the client needs *some* help at all three stages but where the main benefit comes from one more than another. The examples in this and the next chapter relate to clients with real needs at Phase III.

 Rex was referred to a counsellor by a psychiatrist, with the comment that the man was too far removed geographically for the next six months for the psychiatrist to monitor his progress. "What he needs is someone to sit on his head for a couple of hours a week and beat some sense into him."

It did not sound too sympathetic, yet in a sense it was, if for no other reason than that the client totally concurred. "I'm drinking too much, I've lost my licence, and I'm so rebellious about the work that I'm going to get the sack. I need a minder."

Rex had interrupted his career in mid-thirties to go for an advanced degree, in order to improve his future chances. This was his current "work". So the goal was perfectly clear, and the means. He just was not getting on with it and that was where he wanted help. Very much a *Phase III* task. A task, incidentally, not wholly unfamiliar to some managers. Certainly not one which in itself required professional or specialist help.

In this case, even though the task is a Phase III task for the counsellor, she still needed to touch base at Phase I, if only to show she was a good listener, in principle on the client's side.

Phase II also needed some reworking, because the client had partly lost sight of his goal, needed to be challenged to reaffirm his motivation, and needed to be confronted directly about the way he was sabotaging himself. But the main task remained at Phase III, which was to badger and cajole him to follow through on his resolution.

What the counsellor had to do in practice was to get Rex to make out a study schedule which he could stick to; establish checkpoints for this schedule during the term; find out from his fellow students what standard of work they were turning in (they were getting 'A's where he was getting 'C's, yet he had never thought to examine an 'A' essay to compare quality); push him to attend the syndicate meetings and tutorials he was neglecting; make him organize his reading list (he was a voracious reader and was reading too much, writing too little); and so on.

The counsellor's contribution

This example show how the counsellor is more obviously active at the third phase than in the previous two. The gradual increase in the amount of input from the counsellor as counselling moves through the three stages can be shown diagramatically:

Phase I	Phase II	Phase III
	The counsellor's contribution	
Active listening but the client has the lead	The counsellor begins to use his influence	The counsellor is more active and pro-active

This also means that a much wider *range* of input may be required of the counsellor than in the first two phases. And yet the guiding principle of all three phases is preserved, that the client is expected to solve the problem, as far as possible, *out of his own resources.*

The contract

Thus, in Rex's situation, the counsellor did not devise the work schedule *for* him, did not herself approach his assigned tutor (which she in fact was free to do), but got Rex to decide for himself what quality of work was expected, to organize his reading and all the rest. She also got him to phone her twice a week, at prearranged times, apart from the meetings in her office.

The "contract" called for a minder and that was what she did. Further, she put it clearly to Rex that it was indeed a contract.

Almost all forms of counselling and psychotherapy these days talk about having a clear contract between client and counsellor, stating what expectations each may have of the other. Thus, Rex's counsellor was not expected to take complete charge of him, but *was* expected to do so in certain specified areas which Rex agreed to. On his side, he was required to give up drinking completely, to call the counsellor twice a week and at any other time when he realized he was on the verge of sabotaging himself again.

Similarly, in Derek's case, his manager contracted to arrange an advance on his salary, but left it to Derek to work out a repayment system with the accounts department to suit them both. It was also an agreed part of the "deal" that Derek would repair his fences with the customers and colleagues concerned, now that the financial worry was off his shoulders.

> Dividing up the work is a key aspect in the action phase of counselling. At this stage counsellors must be prepared to get their hands dirty. Counselling doesn't begin and end sitting in a chair.

Referring

At the same time, Phase III is pre-eminently the one where the counsellor needs to keep a weather eye open for the temptation to overdo it. We gave two examples of how the work could be split up by mutual agreement, in Rex's case so that the counsellor did not get drawn into doing too much, given Rex's dependent and immature character, and in Derek's case as part of a deal with his boss. Sometimes the counsellor may have to be alert to the need for the work to be shared, not with the client but with another counsellor.

 Pauline is the 50-year old chargehand from Chapter 11. She had successfully undergone surgery for breast cancer. However, she became and remained terribly depressed. She was tearful and complaining, and completely exhausted her friends by her refusal to be cheered up, to the point where they began to avoid her. Which, of course, Pauline noticed and added to her list of complaints. The vicious cycle deepened and her counsellor was first at a loss, then began to cast around for reinforcements.

Pauline herself had given a clue to what she needed by her often repeated: "Nobody really understands what it's like to go through this". Her counsellor discovered that a self-help group of people who had all had bouts with cancer was meeting once a week in the same town. She put Pauline in touch with them and finally things began to improve.

Finally Pauline did believe she was understood. She could no longer claim that her counsellors "didn't know what it's really like". The people in the group were helpful too in small practical ways, and perhaps most important of all asked her to make the first contact with another woman who was facing the same experience but was too nervous to join the group.

Knowing when and how to refer is a major skill in the third phase of counselling. If resourcing the client is the principal contribution at this point and if meeting the client's needs is the major task of counselling in general then the counsellor, to fulfil the task, will need sometimes to be both well informed and creative.

Summary

Phase III is an integral part of the counselling process. That means a number of things, some of which may at first sight appear to be contradictory but which in fact point to the balance which needs to be established between the three phases and between the contributions of the client and the counsellor:

1. The counsellor often does not need to go beyond Phase I, or beyond Phase II.

2. The client may well need to do so, but does not require the counsellor's assistance. The counsellor should be prepared to let the client take charge and depart.

3. Sometimes the client does need the counsellor's continuing assistance at Phase III, may even especially need it at that point. The counsellor may still be the best person for the job and should not bow out, simply because this is called helping rather than counselling, as it may be narrowly defined.

4. Phase III, because of the emphasis on action, is of a very different order to the other two stages, but it keeps the perspective of the whole process in limiting the counsellor's contribution to what clients can't do for themselves.

5. The balance between the three phases and between the contributions of counsellor and client is made more difficult when one or the other works better in (or enjoys) one phase at the expense of another. A counsellor needs to be aware of personal strongpoints and preferences in the different phases.

The emphasis of this chapter has been on the integration of Phase III with the preceding phases, despite its quite different nature. The next chapter puts the emphasis on the different skills required of the counsellor.

17   *THE SKILLS OF PHASE III*

Most books about counselling are inspired (as is this one) by what is called a "client-centred" philosophy. This is sometimes translated as non-directive, where the alternative approach is dubbed directive. The non-directive approach says that the counsellor does not solve the problem for the client, but allows him to tell the story in his own way, meets him with a non-evaluative listening, gently prods him to rethink his position, and so on.

When it comes to Phase III the textbook illustration is of teaching the client a problem-solving method and guiding him through it. I gave a typical example in Chapter 2 with the case of Doris who was determined to give up drinking. This showed how she was helped to develop options and more options, to sift them, to arrange and sequence intermediate goals, to organize the means, to program changes in her normal behaviour, and to arrange for feedback and monitoring procedures. A similar situation was described in the last chapter where Rex, a middle-aged businessman, was failing to get to grips with the postgraduate study programme he had embarked on.

WHAT DOES THE CLIENT NEED?

There is no quarrel with all this. Only that for some clients it is not exactly what they need. In the business and organizational context in particular it will soon seem to lack focus, because issues have to be faced and resolved, actions have to be taken within certain time limits. Clients can't always be left to a self-directed, self-paced process.

In that situation the contribution of the counsellor in Phase III is one of *resourcing* and *servicing* the client to achieve a specific goal.

This is where the perspective of this book parts company with the classic model, without, I believe, betraying its philosophy. If what the client needs is direction, and the counsellor has the experience and authority, then it seems perfectly client-centred to give it to him. It does not imediately produce a directive counsellor, except in so far as it is useful for the client on a particular occasion to be directed. There are plenty of caveats in these pages to demonstrate that such directiveness is best supported by some highly *non*-directive work at Phases I and II.

The resources which a client is likely to be lacking at this point in the process are:

energy/conviction
knowledge/direction.

Hence the counsellor would rightly be more active than in the previous phases, may seize the initiative more readily, may more overtly seek to influence, encourage and support, may push quite openly for commitment.

At this point the counsellor may even wish to exert a certain amount of authority, an authority gained through sensitive work at the earlier stages. Note that I say authority, not power. Once power comes into the picture, counselling goes out of the window. Authority is personal authority, not hierarchical. It is based on better information, knowledge, understanding, on greater experience, objectivity and expertise.

To supplement the client's resources in terms of energy, conviction and commitment, of direction and knowledge, the counsellor may call on a wide range of skills. This chapter picks out six of them which in practice are most common:

- ☐ coaching
- ☐ giving feedback
- ☐ advising
- ☐ offering expertise
- ☐ referring
- ☐ rendering a service.

Coaching

The cases of Doris (Chapter 3) and Rex (Chapter 16) already illustrate this aspect of Phase III skills. Doris' counsellor fulfilled the role more as a guide through a problem-solving sequence, Rex's counsellor acted more as a minder. Another instance shows a different aspect of the role.

Virginia is a 22-year old secretary. She feels that her boss is over-familiar with her, but is afraid she may lose her job if she tells him she is unhappy with the way he is behaving.

No doubt the counsellor will want Virginia to clear her feelings about the situation (Phase I) and will also anticipate some re-examination of her thinking which apparently leaves her unsure of her basic rights as a woman. But quite probably, when she comes to the point of confronting her boss, she will need some *coaching,* some rehearsal of how exactly she is going to put it, what she will do next depending on how he reacts.

Giving feedback

As was the case in isolating the separate skills of Phase II, those of Phase III may partly overlap. Even so, the examples show different facets.

 Tony drove his fellow board members up the wall. Within his own technical function he was highly regarded, but when it came to making presentations or arguing a case he made a fool of himself. The managing director had got him to attend presentation skills and relaxation courses, which made little difference, and finally persuaded him to see a counsellor.

The counsellor got Tony to talk easily enough because he himself was quite determined to do something about it. Apart from anything else he had reached the top of his own particular functional ladder and if he were to go any higher he would have to move sideways into general management, a position he would never be offered unless he could learn to behave differently.

Like many clients, Tony was aware enough of the curious way he slipped into this behaviour and soon related it to a standard scene from his childhood where a very articulate father was standing over him, saying: "Well, come on lad – spit it out!", leading predictably to stammering and incoherence.

Just this much exploration was enough to provoke a shift in Tony's thinking (Phase II) and the counsellor moved on to Phase III. One can hang around for a long time in Phase II, redoing a client's early years. With counsellors and clients who are highly analytical it is easy to be self-indulgent at this point, without, however, making much progress. But this counsellor knew that a bit of success from some constructive work at Phase III can also have a reassuring rebound effect on Phase II. Sometimes it is tactically sounder to push through all three phases, get a limited result, and then go back for more.

In any case Tony's contract with his counsellor was for remedial work at Phase III, not to analyse why he was the way he was, even though the counsellor happened to be quite skilful in analytic work.

So they moved on to Phase III and picked apart what Tony actually *did* with presentations. What he did was next to nothing. Given that he was not anticipating it to be a particularly rewarding event he prepared only hastily at the last minute. As it happened, one of Tony's annual major presentations was due two weeks after his first meeting with the counsellor, who quickly switched to a coaching-training mode (Phase III) and temporarily abandoned Phases I and II. The result was a resounding success, private and public praise from the MD. Round one to the counsellor.

Round two was about board meetings. Tony and the counsellor set up a discussion between themselves and recorded it on audio tape. Tony listened to the recording and said:
"I talk an awful lot, don't I?"
"Yes" [said the counsellor] "you talk a lot. If you listen again you will hear that the reason is you qualify everything with so many riders and parentheses that even *you* have forgotten the main point long before you get to the end. Let's play it back and this time you insert the full stops, shorten the sentences, and focus on what your partner actually wants to know – rather than on all the things you think you need to say. There are a couple of things, too, which you won't pick up because they are visual. One is that you offer your partner a series of grins when there is nothing funny, and the other is that periodically you drop eye-contact. You actually look sideways and slightly up. When that happens, it is as though you go into an internal loop. Whenever that happens I know I've lost you. Or rather you have lost contact with me. I could sit here in front of you for five minutes picking my nose and you wouldn't know."

Typically, Tony did not know he did those things. Nobody had ever told him he smiled inappropriately, or that his eye-contact wandered so much. He was amazed when he started catching himself doing it. But he did start catching himself, caught himself looking away and yanked his eyes back. Suddenly his sentences started getting shorter, suddenly his opposite number began to see the chance for a dialogue, instead of being audience to a monologue.

It perhaps goes without saying that the counsellor's feedback was acceptable because of the confidence, trust and credit he had built up with Tony. It is at Phase III that the counsellor has sometimes to take the risk of cashing all his credit with the client. But if he has done a careful job at the first two phases his chances are a lot better than evens.

Advising

Tony provides a good example of advising too, because at the end of their ten sessions he asked the counsellor if he had any further recommendations. The counsellor had been of the private opinion from the beginning that Tony had been sent on the wrong courses. With an open invitation to offer advice he recommended Tony would benefit more and make further progress by signing up for assertiveness training. He also gave him some leads to find out where such courses were held.

Clients make quite legitimate requests for feedback and recommendations. Some counsellors back off hastily in the face of such demands: "You are interested in what I think, are you? Hm, that's interesting – I wonder why . . . ?" This is taking non-directiveness too far.

I am asked, from time to time, in private coaching sessions "How do I come across?" (as manager, negotiator, counsellor, salesman) "to you?" People are not asking for interpretation or in-depth analysis, simply how they come across. It is a perfectly reasonable request, they are genuinely open to comment, the situation is completely protected and they are almost always grateful, often relieved at the response. So why not say what I think? I have learned over the years to follow the rules of good feedback – to be specific and behavioural, rather than personal, to be concrete rather than interpretative, to be impressionistic only if pushed, to point to consequences of behaviour as well as to the behaviour itself, to make only tentative suggestions about alternative courses of action, and so on.

Using experience. There are other contexts, too, in which advice and recommendations from the counsellor are appropriate. "My advice is that in the long run you would do better to apply for retraining sooner rather than later", says the union rep. It is not an either–or situation, either counselling or directive advice, but rather that the latter builds on the former, that either may be the more appropriate at different moments.

Phase III is the stage where the counsellor's experience may be greater, where he or she from a broader base of similar cases can say that one alternative has normally been shown to be the better. One can listen to a tax adviser lay out the various options in a non-directive way, or listen to the union rep. outlining alternative tactics; but in the end one will want to say: OK I see all that but what would *you* do in the same situation? And the client expects an unequivocal answer.

The patient will listen to the dentist set out the choices he has but will still want to know what the dentist thinks is best. In this and similar cases the client only wants to be sure first that the special nature of the problems he faces, his own particular case, has been properly evaluated alongside all the other cases the "expert" has seen until now. He only wants to make sure the dentist is talking about *his* teeth and not teeth in general. That will be assured by the listening and probing of the first two phases which will also have guided the *client* to ask the right question.

At this point one is talking of influencing skills as much as counselling. No one, however, has a better basis for acquiring influence with a client than the good counsellor. One text on counselling is written entirely round the thesis that the process is simply one of gaining and then *using* influence with a client for the client's benefit.

Offering expertise

This is a wider category than the previous one. Advice is based on expertise, but expertise itself is based on knowledge, information and experience. An expert is not necessarily some form of *qualified* specialist. The personnel officer is not always a specialist in that sense, but he or she might well have knowledge about company policy and practices, information about future perspectives, experience of similar situations in other companies or longstanding acquaintance with the present one. In that sense he or she has expertise.

The same is true of some specialist counsellors, even though again they may lack formal qualifications. Pauline was seen in the last chapter getting the best help simply from people who had been through the same experience and had had more time to digest it. In that sense, though completely unqualified, they were specialists and experts.

Specialist counselling. The reason why we have specialist counsellors at all – probation officers, career counsellors, marriage counsellors, sex therapists, drug counsellors, alcohol counsellors, bereavement counsellors and so on – is that they *know* more than the average client.

The career counsellor is expected to know where the right jobs are, which are the right jobs for different people, how to approach prospective employers and so on. Drug or alcohol abuse counsellors know a lot about these substances – what they actually contain, what their effects are in different doses, what the course and pace of addiction is likely to be, what specialized treatment programmes may be available and their cost.

A marriage counsellor may be expected to know what the least painful/ costly method of separation or divorce has been found to be, what to tell the children, what the likely chances are of the marriage surviving.

These experts have "seen it all before" and have some sort of chart or framework in their heads which enables them to correctly place you (diagnose you) the client, and then tell you what your chances are.

> As well as being in a position to offer advice in Phase III of counselling specialist counsellors are often in a better position to *confront* in Phase II. Confrontation comes better from the perceived expert. He or she is well placed to say (to the addict or the alcoholic, for example) "Sorry, that doesn't wash. It's a tale I've heard too often, and every addict who gets cured comes back and tells me the best thing I ever did for them was not to let them get away with blaming somebody else for their problem."

The marriage counsellor may be able to say:

> *"You know, just about every person on the verge of separation takes it for granted they are the injured party. Let me know when you are ready to sing a different song. Otherwise it would be simpler to get straight to a lawyer."*

I would hope the average counsellor does not talk like this as a matter of course, but there are occasions when it is the right thing to do, when the counsellor is sure he has understood correctly and when, tactically, a sharp challenge can break the logjam. This is the proper use of expertise. If it is timed well clients will take it willingly. They may even tell their friends proudly how the counsellor "straightened me out", "told it me like it is".

Such confrontation is acceptable because the client is sure the counsellor knows what he is talking about.

Referring

If this is a relatively short section it is not because this is an unimportant skill. I have already made the point that some counsellors too quickly abandon their clients at Phase III. But on the other side there are those who stick with a client through thick and thin to the point where they stray hopelessly beyond the boundaries of their competence, to say nothing of their comfort. One company counsellor was suddenly told by her client that he was a transvestite. She had no idea how to deal with the situation, was even somewhat confused what the difference was between a transvestite and a homosexual. She felt she was trapped because it had been said in confidence. But in purely practical terms she was unable to be of much help, should have said she was out of her depth and asked him if she might refer him to another counsellor (equally in confidence) who was more experienced.

 Sandy is a young bank auditor. She goes around from branch to branch and writes a report. But lately she has been turning in her reports late, not arriving on time for Monday morning briefings, claiming (falsely) that documents must have gone astray in the post, and so on.

Again, the company had an internal counsellor. This time the counsellor acknowledged that he had run out of ideas with Sandy. There was something wrong which he couldn't quite put his finger on. He referred the girl to a local clinical psychologist.

Indeed there was something wrong. Sandy had had depressive episodes in her teens, there was a depressive history in other members of her immediate family, she had always had a very competitive relationship with one of her sisters. In the past she had run away; she had once dozed off at the wheel of a car. She was again showing signs of an impending crisis, and with her own agreement was hospitalized – possibly just in time – for a period of four weeks, to deal with an acute depressive episode. The company counsellor simply did not have the personal or professional resources to cope. He rightly referred Sandy to an expert.

If the central skill of Phase III is to supplement the client's resources, if there is a role at this stage for the expert, qualified or unqualified, then counsellors must be ready to supplement their own resources too, and be ready to look for expertise they themselves don't have.

Rendering a service

If the range of help counsellors might supply in this last stage of counselling is already wide, then the range of concrete services they might need to furnish is wider still.

It might mean simply writing a letter to the authorities for someone who is not very handy with words. It might mean calling an agency, tracking down a piece of missing information, changing a work schedule, checking with a colleague who might offer the client a different job, arranging for funds. The manager-counsellor is in a particularly strong position here because he or she may have the power to make something happen – which is rarely the case with the independent counsellor. These examples and the one that follows are only a sample of the scores of services which are possible.

 Geoff has been struggling with writing a CV. He is in the middle of changing jobs, has been to see a career counsellor and cooperated as fully as he can. John, the counsellor, keeps turning down Geoff's attempts at a CV, and finally roars: "Leave the damn thing to me", and in an hour comes back with a much improved version. Geoff gets on with the next round of approaches to prospective employers and immediately begins to receive positive replies and job interviews.

Summary

Phase Three of the counselling process is about supplementing the client's resources to reach a specified goal. The examples of this and the preceding chapter demonstrate the range of activities in which the counsellor may become engaged. Clients may need their energy, conviction, motivation and commitment reinforcing. They may lack the experience, knowledge or expertise to take them forward. This may involve the counsellor in coaching, giving feedback, advising and recommending, using his own expertise, referring to other kinds of expertise or just performing a simple service which the client cannot do for himself.

One of the areas of counselling which is dependent on Phase III skills, on a specialized knowledge base, is that of redundancy counselling. The next chapter uses it as a single extended example of counselling which goes through all three phases but calls particularly upon the skills of the third.

18 PHASE III EXAMPLE – REDUNDANCY COUNSELLING

The last chapter illustrated the wide variety of ways in which a counsellor might continue to help a client in Phase III. Because the possible range is so enormous it is difficult to offer a single extended example of Phase III work which might be considered typical, as I do with the first two phases. There is, however, one area of counselling which is enjoying a growing popularity and which serves the same purpose rather well.

The advertised weight of redundancy counselling, certainly in the case of the professional outplacement firms, lies in Phase III – getting someone a new job.

Interestingly, if one watches what they actually do, it normally involves all three phases. In practice, their procedures closely mirror the sequence and style of the general counselling model I have been describing. In-company redundancy counsellors can adapt these procedures to fit the needs of their own organization. But for the purposes of this chapter I focus on specialist outplacement agencies. They illustrate the classic sequence of counselling procedures and allow me to take one final look at the total process.

Also, while so much of the book is written to encourage the ordinary individual to think of himself as potentially able to help many other ordinary people, I want to note the other side of the coin, which is the "expert" role in some areas of counselling.

It is here that the counsellor may also play the role of consultant – the one that people sometimes confuse with counselling and which new counsellors are tempted to play too soon.

■ ■ ■ ■

OUTPLACEMENT CAREER COUNSELLING

Apart from differences in packaging, optional extras and philosophy (which can add up to quite a lot of difference, just as they can with motor cars) the *sequence* followed by any of the major redundancy counselling agencies is basically the same. That is, it will start with an appraisal session or sessions, moves into what is commonly called a "marketing" phase and ends with an attack on the job market. The three segments are quite similar to the three phases we have outlined for all types of counselling.

In the first phase the client explains himself to the counsellor. The counsellor's sole job is to understand the client as a unique individual; and some time may have to be spent initially in debriefing a client who is experiencing the hitherto unique situation of being out of work, whether "voluntarily" or not. A lot of listening is required of the counsellor.

At this point the counsellor will have to go as slowly as the client's feelings allow. Resentment, sadness and anxiety are typically dominating realities. Plus, sometimes, excitement, liberation and enthusiasm. None are guaranteed to help the individual think clearly and rationally, and the goal of this phase, as usual, remains largely one of *CLARIFICATION*, of separating feeling from thinking, of defining the issues, for the client. And for the counsellor it means *UNDERSTANDING*, through drawing out the story.

In the second segment one of the major aims may well be to *CHANGE* the client's self-concept. Indeed, one may say that the client who is simply looking for a switch from a post in one organization to a mirror image in another scarcely needs counselling, as it has been defined in this book. So the work of this middle stage is typically one of *REDEFINING* the problem. Clients must no longer think of themselves as failed sales/marketing people from corporate headquarters in the south-east, looking for something similar among Thames Valley neighbours. They begin to think of themselves as having experience relevant to advertising or journalism, perhaps on a network basis, anywhere between Bristol, Birmingham and London, with potentially higher risks and earnings. Quite a switch in thinking.

With the re-thinking and re-evaluation of Phase II complete, clients are now ready for the third segment. The goal all along has been to get them in front of prospective employers. This is where the final version of the CV (which has been growing in shape and style as the clients begin to see themselves differently) is edited; this is where various techniques of scouring the job market are put into operation – sifting the ads, deluging the search and recruitment agencies, targetting prime companies; this is where letters are composed and sent; where clients are taken through a number of rehearsals for each interview and debriefed after them; where morale may need a periodic boost when the market seems deaf to their cries.

This is the period when the problem is finally *MANAGED*, no longer needing to be clarified or redefined. This is where the counsellor has to draw on

RESOURCING skills rather than on listening or challenging, though these retain their importance in the background.

Typically, of course, the phases of counselling do not follow each other smoothly as though on rails. In all forms of counselling there is stop and go, a mixture of phases, back-tracking and lurching forward. The professional career counsellor will quite likely begin work on the CV right from the beginning, may *instruct* the client (a Phase III skill) to begin networking immediately. In practice, as in general counselling, there is often an overlap and repetition of the different stages over any period of time.

Going to the expert

Redundancy or, as many prefer to call it, *career* counselling is popular partly because it meets a need for expertise. Clients like it because it can shortcut their own uninformed efforts and bring them more quickly to a solution. Career counsellors like it (or some of them do) because it gives them the security of the expert position, of providing a specialized service, of a broader knowledge. Career counsellors know something their clients do not know. For example, they know how to present a good image both on paper and at interview. They can coach people in the necessary skills.

Then they have a much wider database than the average individual could hope to have. As a minimum they will have *Executive Grapevine* on computer. They have built up a series of contacts, both formal and informal, into a mesh of routes which the job-seeker might take. They are reputed even to have the entree to that Mecca of unemployed executives – the "unadvertised job market". And last, but not least, they have back-up services, such as library, office and secretarial help. You may be able to have your own desk in their office and certainly you will be able to turn out impeccable documents on the word-processor. All giving you an edge on your fellows who are trying to do it on their own.

Differences in emphasis

This liking for expertise leads some career counselling agencies to put too much reliance on it. They make a baton charge on the third phase, will do practically everyting *for* the client on the grounds that this is what they are paid for. They may be shorter on listening skills, longer or encouragement, chivvying and advice. Some will use tests and measurement as a matter of course, relish the professionalism which such procedures represent. Others believe they can get at the relevant personality variables in a surer way through the counselling process itself.

These are the ones who may be drawn to put a premium on the counselling of the first phase, with the philosophy that, once the groundwork is in place, the shift in thinking of the second phase may even bring the client to consider hitherto unimagined options – maybe even continuing employment in the present company or group.

As well as the variations between agencies, individual counsellors, as we saw in Chapter 16, may well have their preferences for one phase or another. Some seem to feel safer when they enter the zone of expertise and can coach, instruct, and deploy an armoury of tools, techniques, information and services. Others are stronger on the more personal aspects of the first two phases, and may find the meticulous work of the third rather boring; it takes them beyond their range of comfort. Others again blend the various elements quite skilfully, or they separate them by referring clients to different consultants for each stage, within the group.

Finally, of course, if the emphasis changes from agency to agency, and from counsellor to counsellor, *clients* too will vary in their preferences, expectations and motivation. Some will not want to sit still for what they see as a protracted review of their career, talents and interests; others will be grateful for the chance of a more thoughtful and leisurely overhaul of their motivation and perspectives.

Choosing the right career counsellor may well be the first and most important decision the out-of-work executive will make.

IN-COMPANY REDUNDANCY COUNSELLING

There is room for the dedicated career/redundancy counsellor within an organization to acquire some of the expertise of the external agency. Such a counsellor can legitimately be expected to have a wider database than the client: to know more about company manpower projections and opportunities, to have a wider perspective and array of options, to be able to direct the client to other sources of information, to make recommendations, to make referrals to specialized sources of assistance. That will be what some clients need and what they can rightly expect.

At the same time, the generic counsellors for whom this text is primarily written – line managers, administrators, technicians working for customers, personnel and training officers – are more often in a situation which allows for much less of the kind of expertise which career counsellors can bring to bear at the third, or action, phase. Part of the perspective presented here is to demonstrate that in the majority of cases expertise is *not* what is needed, that the sorts of situation which arise on a daily basis within an organization can effectively be dealt with at the first two phases, perhaps even only at the first.

David is a case in point. He came for help to find a new job. He had run a number of companies but had been out of work for nine months. He had been moping for nine months, very hurt at the way he had been engineered out of his last assignment, apprehensive that his forthright style would put him into conflict with new colleagues or bosses: suddenly, at 52, unsure of himself.

He met a counsellor seven times over the space of four months. It was the first time he had been able to talk freely about his sense of failure, relate it spontaneously to the feelings of inadequacy of his seven-year old self who had had to play the role of the man about the house, when father did not return from the war and mother could not cope with the troublesome behaviour of his younger sister.

The outcome of their discussions was that David began to perceive and understand himself differently, more realistically, less critically and to see how his aggressiveness had been used to mask his uncertainty. At the end of the four months David was actively looking for jobs, indeed turned up quite a range of options, entirely on his own initiative.

A colleague commented that he sounded sure of himself again, and his wife, who had been sceptical about counselling, came to acknowledge that David had changed quite noticeably.

What was interesting from the counsellor's point of view was that David had moved into the action phase by himself. Indeed he refused to let the counsellor get too involved at that point. He needed to do it himself and wouldn't even consider going to a professional career counselling organization. He seemed to know exactly what he wanted from the counsellor, which was to remain as a source of encouragement and support. Someone who had understood him without criticising but was also willing to challenge when necessary.

In the third phase he would only accept the counsellor's insistence that the job openings he had turned up for himself be systematically sifted in terms of his short and long term

goals, and added the wry footnote: "You know, I wouldn't
have let anyone else force me to be so rational". It was no
special knowledge or expertise that David wanted. It was the
long and patient work at Phase I which did the trick.

Summary

*This chapter illustrates the twin themes of the book. It has first taken the
example of redundancy counselling as one which exemplifies the need for
expertise in some situations and in some areas of counselling.*

*At the same time it has re-emphasized a central theme, that the other factor
in good counselling is the non-expert position of the listener at Phase I and
Phase II, and that this is the safest underpinning for any kind of expertise. A
parallel theme is that when it comes to the day-to-day problems which
interfere with people's productiveness and energy, most of them do not
require an expert. For most of such problems there is not a specialized
"database" which a counsellor needs. Most day-to-day counselling by the
manager, the colleague, the administrator, the spouse can take a person
through all three phases of counselling simply by understanding the
problem, putting it into a shape where some conclusion is possible, then
guiding the person through the choices needed to put it into operation.*

*And of course there is the constant need for support or encouragement
when people are making changes. The value of support cannot be
overestimated. Just "being" there is sometimes the best way people can and
do help each other.*

SECTION THREE

Counselling and the Organization

An approach which was developed in the context of an individual presenting himself with his problems to another, who has no other systematic relationship with him, hierarchical or otherwise, may be expected to take on another cast when it is translated into commerce, industry and service organizations.

Chapter 19 looks at the ways in which the organization's goals may be in conflict with the individual's, and how this discrepancy will affect the way in which counselling, as outlined in the previous section, can be translated into the context of the organization. It also examines how this conflict is reflected in the way organizations define and use the term "counselling", and the benefits they look for in it.

Chapter 20 picks out and examines several aspects of the role conflict which individual managers may experience in the counselling situation, and suggests ways of viewing and dealing with them.

Chapter 21 gives guidelines for setting up in-company employee counselling services.

19   THE CONTEXT OF COUNSELLING

I have been at some pains in the latter part of this book to stress two things:
1. *That counselling issues naturally into the third phase of consulting, coaching, advising, servicing and resourcing.*
2. *That these processes, to be successful, will normally be underpinned by counselling in its earlier phases.*

■ ■ ■ ■

MUTUAL INTEREST OR CONFLICT?

Where the independent counsellor is helping a client there is no conflict of interest because, once the contract between the two is agreed, the process is designed to satisfy only the interests of the client.

It is important for organization counsellors, managers or anybody, to recognize that employers have a legitimate concern with performance. There will be an emphasis on Phase III – action: positive change, measurable results. The third phase of counselling is extremely important in business and industry. There is likely to be some impatience with a model which runs out of steam after Phase I, or Phase II.

It is equally important that organizations recognize that counselling skills, as they have been outlined here, also imply certain attitudes and beliefs about people, that these attitudes are an essential part of what counselling is intended to convey, and also that as the term "counselling" has grown in public awareness, it has sometimes been adopted in a sense which may distort that essential meaning.

THE MEANING OF COUNSELLING

If I am being insistent on this point it is because the way that the word and concept of counselling is used or understood within a particular company will determine what the goals of counselling may be, how it is practised, and to what extent (or even whether) the model of counselling presented here is possible.

One overhears, for example, comments such as: "I counselled him to . . .", where the correct word would be "advised"; or "What she needs is a good dose of counselling", where the (praiseworthy) aim is apparently to make a reprimand more palatable, but where the possibility of counselling in the sense used in this book becomes rather unlikely. One company teaches the tentative and tactful confrontation skills used in Phase II under the heading "rattle and shake". A recent book on listening skills, technically quite good and destined for the business market, recommends that the listener focuses attention through the question: "What's in it for *me*?" And so on. None of these usages of the word would fit easily into the approach outlined here.

I recently surveyed some 20 companies, and found that the majority use counselling in the context of performance review, both formal (appraisal) and informal. The approach seems to be inspired in one way or another by the idea that the employee may have something to contribute to the proper evaluation of his or her own work and may then be more open to corrective action.

Some use counselling as part of their training methods, again so that trainees may have the opportunity to assess their individual strengths and weaknesses.

The term is also commonly used in the context of "career counselling" and "redundancy counselling", where the meaning most closely approaches that adopted here, as does its use, for example, by a couple of UK airlines to describe the process of debriefing flight crews who have been under pressure.

Other companies use counselling as part of the disciplinary procedure, sometimes mandatory, sometimes not.

We are here in the swirling and muddy waters of company philosophy, policy and politics. One respondent to the survey considered the inclusion of "counselling" in the disciplinary process in his own organization to be a purely defensive manoeuvre, designed to portray the company as caring.

WHO OWNS THE PROBLEM?

If counselling is about helping the individual to solve a problem, two radically different perspectives may be encapsulated in the question: "Who owns the problem?"

If the company is concerned solely to show itself as caring, then the assumption is that the employee is the real owner of the problem, and is therefore uniquely responsible, in the last analysis, for its solution. Counselling, however, in the sense that it is used in this book, implies that it is a service for people who have a problem, who accept ownership of the problem but who need help to solve it. That means that the organization accepts partial responsibility for the solution, if not the problem. There is of course the further possibility that, once an organization accepts that it may be well placed to help with solutions, it may be forced to the recognition that, in some cases, it is contributing to the problems.

This may well be one reason why "counselling" has acquired such a plethora of nuances in so short a time. Some of them are clearly a distortion of the meaning given to it in this book and quite easily give rise to the perception that it is simply another management ploy – witness the rather cynical comment quoted above – offered for the company's benefit, not the employee's. The perspective which underpins the whole of the foregoing is that counselling needs to be offered unequivocally for the employee's benefit.

"Unequivocally" does not mean that one must be misty-eyed. Companies are not of their nature altruistic and should not be expected to be so. But "for the employee's benefit" does not necessarily mean *against* the organization's interest. The two are not incompatible. Companies may be persuaded that altruism pays. Though they do not exist to offer contentment to their employees, many are already persuaded that employee satisfaction is reflected in the bottom line. Chapter 21 explores this issue in more detail.

Summary

This chapter has been concerned with the possibility of conflict between the goals of the organization and those of the individual, and has sought to reconcile them. While the weight of the book has been on counselling skills, it is recognized that such skills are deployed within the context of an organization which (rightly) places legitimate expectations on its employees. They, in their turn, have problems which impact on their performance. The question is: who has real ownership of these problems?

The whole of this book is predicated on the premiss that people will not solve their problems until they accept their share of ownership. On the other side, the organization can sometimes provide help with the solution. Not only that but the organization may be, in some cases, the ultimate source of the problem. It may play a significant role, for good or ill. Some of the ills it may cause or cure.

In the last chapter we look at the way in which a number of companies have systematically applied themselves to providing such help. That means that while they have accepted some responsibility for helping employees with problems which impact on their work (for highly pragmatic reasons), the question remains untouched as to what extent some of these problems are provoked by the conditions and environment which the organization offers. That is a matter of Organization Development which this book does not presume to address at any length. Not that such issues are irrelevant. At the very least, Chapter 17 on Phase III skills will alert the reader to management's opportunity to exert the executive power it possesses to change the circumstances which are the seedbed of some of its employees' problems.

In the meantime Chapter 20 focuses more sharply on how the individual manager may be caught up in the discrepancy between individual and organizational goals, and how that may engage him or her in a variety of role conflicts.

20   ROLE CONFLICT IN COUNSELLING

*The possibility of role conflict for counsellors in organizations has been
touched on in previous pages. This chapter looks at the matter more
systematically. The root of the difficulties which managers and supervisors
may experience can be traced to certain ambiguities in the situation of the
manager-as-counsellor. The same ambiguities are shared to a certain extent by
those who have staff rather than line responsibilities.*

■ ■ ■ ■

**First, managers and supervisors carry a natural responsibility to
evaluate, control and improve performance.**

The company's objectives demand it, the way they carry it out is part of what
they themselves are assessed on. Such pressures, from above and below,
make middle management one of the most stressed groups in an
organization. The calm listening, the reassurance and basic compassion of
the counsellor are difficult to come by. The manager cannot refrain from
making decisions, from passing judgment.

Ian Hoare (in an article in *Counselling,* May 1984) relates the telling example
of a group of managers he trained in listening skills, to the point where they
were tolerably good at it and wholly convinced of its value. They were then
given situations to deal with where performance was part of the issue, when
lo and behold, to their own dismay, they forgot all about listening. They
were no longer sure if listening was even possible.

The manager and the counsellor may easily have different priorities. A
manager may need to confront where the relatively independent counsellor
can afford to wait for the person to confront himself. The counsellor can
perhaps afford to accept any one of three solutions to a problem, but the
manager may have to insist on only one. He or she may have to insist on one
particular result, one outcome, however much freedom the individual is
given to choose the means. The counsellor can usually be more relaxed
about goals as well as means.

The gulf between the two perspectives may sometimes seem too wide to
bridge. One might say that the counsellor works *for* the client, the employee
works *for* the manager-counsellor. But this is to overdraw the difference in

perspective. All sorts of people in authority have the same situation, the same dilemma. Teachers, nurses and, of course, parents play a significant management role with their charges. But they shift just as often into a helping, caring, counselling role too.

Likewise the manager may play now one and now the other. What has often been missing from the manager's own education is *training* in counselling. Hence this book, which underlines at once both the techniques and the attitudes of good counselling. But the last thing it is intended to do is to shackle managers in their main duty – to manage. It is intended to show how they may do both at different times – and incidentally enhance their authority as managers.

Second, people often come to a manager because there is something or other he can do for them, there is something in his gift, so to speak.

They are not there for counselling at all. They are only interested in Phase III – action. They *want* something. They want a Yes or a No. Can they or can they not extend their sick leave, have a rise, go on flexitime, change their client-base, postpone a deadline?

From the typical counsellor's point of view this may be an enviable position. The independent counsellor usually does not have the executive power to bring about a change in the situation which will be beneficial to the client. Managers sometimes do. They can sometimes nip a problem in the bud simply by doing something. They may not need to counsel. If it makes sense they may simply say: Yes, you can (. . . go on flexitime, or whatever). They can arrange matters where the simple counsellor cannot.

One way this book may be useful is in helping the manager decide when to counsel and when not. George the foreman is asking if he can postpone a deadline. "There is no way we can get the stuff out on time", he says.

There is one kind of George who, when he says he can't get the stuff out on time, means he has run into unexpected problems which he will sort out with the minimum delay, but the manager is being given early warning that he will have to do some reshuffling on his own account.

There is another kind of George who cannot meet a deadline because he cannot organize his workforce properly. Perhaps they fall behind because George likes to handle all machine breakdowns himself. Perhaps that is what he likes to do best. Maybe he thinks the men respect him most for his technical skill, and is afraid he would lose their loyalty and respect if he did not continue to get his hands dirty. This George needs counselling before he needs managing.

Third, the employee does not start by *owning* the problem.

George, the foreman in the previous example, does not actually think he has a problem. He believes there *is* a problem but he isn't part of it. Maybe it is the manager – for setting impossible targets. Perhaps it is the "new generation" of operatives who don't have (and never will have) the mechanical know-how to look after their own machines. He doesn't see that his own expertise came through experience, by being allowed to try things, by being shown, by experimenting, by learning.

He does not see there is anything he can do about the problem. That is why people say: if you are not part of the solution you *are* part of the problem. But George does not see it that way. He does not "own" the problem.

The manager's first task is often to *give* it to him. Counselling is a delicate enough process. To need first to convince someone that they *have* a problem is even more so. This is typically the case with performance issues.

The redundancy counsellor too may face the same paradox. He or she is easily seen as the agent of the organization which has *given* the person their problem, and can be the natural recipient of the welter of feelings which are involved – panic, resentment, bewilderment, grief.

One may spare a thought in passing for the in-company redundancy counsellor. It can be an intensely demoralizing and conflict-provoking task, if it is not further complicated by the knowledge that theirs will be the next jobs to go. Professional counsellors are brought up to the recognition that they themselves need counselling from time to time. In-company counsellors often go without such support. Nor have they had experience and training to recognize and deal with the burden of other people's feelings, not to take them home with them, but rather to find ways of unloading them, as their professional colleagues usually can.

The manager, too, if he is to go behind the surface problem will have to face the more emotional upheaval of dealing with the problem *behind* it. George's real problem will not go away until his manager tackles it head-on. From a stress point of view that will be more demanding for the manager. He too may need some help. And maybe that is *his* real problem. He does not like asking for it.

Fourth, of course, is the issue of confidentiality.

The reason most often given by employees why they are reluctant to accept counselling from anybody in the organization, even where there is no line relationship, is that they cannot be sure that what they reveal will not in some way prejudice their employment, either now or in the future.

Managers in their turn may want to refuse confidences because they are not sure they could maintain an unprejudiced personal attitude or an uncontaminated judgment of the individual from the company's point of view. Quite reasonably they may be afraid of having their hands tied, wittingly or unwittingly, by an employee's openness about a personal problem.

> One personnel manager I know is quite clear in her own mind which "hat" she is wearing, and when talking with someone makes it quite clear which one it is. But most people are afraid that what they have under their hats may leak unwanted into their heads.

Fifth is the ambiguity of the situation.

The individual manager is a caring person, but company culture, policy or procedures are geared in such a way that he or she is restricted from the outset in terms of the help they may offer. Such people may hesitate to get involved where the only response open to them is a kind of impotent sympathy which would leave them feeling all the more frustrated.

Sixth is a more fundamental factor which makes some people frankly unwilling to be involved in the counselling role.

They may hide behind a protest about the kind of ambiguities just discussed but in fact it is more a question of personal *ambivalence* than role ambiguity. This may be for a variety of reasons:

- [ ] some people simply do not have a natural sympathy, warmth or caring for others

- [ ] some would rather describe themselves as "pragmatic", by which they mean they set little store by feelings

- [ ] some nourish the conviction that people (i.e. other people) are basically lazy or inept

- [ ] some see counselling as encouraging malingerers rather than building trust and loyalty.

Seventh is another kind of ambivalence which is rooted in the genuine difficulty of good listening.

One aspect of it is the struggle anyone will experience when his or her own emotions or values are engaged by what someone is saying. Most of us can really only pay attention to one thing at a time. If our own vested interests are being challenged (however unknowingly) by the other person, we do not normally keep the focus of our attention on what they are actually saying. Good listening – for whatever purpose, be it counselling, negotiating or managing – needs to become second nature if we are not to become entangled in our own reactions.

> A second and related aspect of this genuine difficulty in listening is that for many people there is something inherently competitive about talking. If someone tells me they nearly went under a bus, what is the most common reaction? I want to tell them the same thing happened to me. Most people don't listen for long before they start to itch to get in their own two pennyworth.

There may be something here, something even more basic in many people, which is a *reluctance* to listen, from the belief that if they listen they may be forced to agree, that if they see the other's point of view they may have to give up their own.

In fact is is not true, but I have seen it everywhere. Not just with managers, but with negotiators. Not just in the boardroom, but in the bedroom. Listening is felt to be the same as giving in. If there is anything competitive in a relationship between two people there will be a conflict or a struggle about listening. The struggle is about making sure the other listens *first*. "I'll go in and tell him when he's ready to listen", says the employee. And the boss? "I'll listen to him when he changes his tune".

Summary and conclusion

In this chapter I have been looking at the ambiguities and genuine difficulties which people experience with counselling where there are role relationships between counsellor and client.

I have also been suggesting that for these reasons some people will rarely be in the right frame of mind to engage successfully in counselling until they come to grips with their ambivalence and begin to listen better.

But among those who do, even the most "pragmatic" manager will come to see that better listening (Phase I), more tactful challenging (Phase II), and more generous assistance (Phase III), actually pays off in terms of results. And as such a person's skills increase, perhaps some of the underlying attitudes may also come to be further modified.

We might however close the chapter by taking the spotlight away from the manager, supervisor, administrator. He or she is a useful focal point for examining the role conflicts which counselling inside an organization may provoke. However, I have been illustrating the point throughout these pages that counselling in an organization is not the manager's prerogative. It is a role which anyone may take, colleagues and friends included.

In many companies it also forms a significant part of the personnel function; in some cases counselling has been systematically introduced by them as a company-wide service, available to provide help with personal problems to any employee (sometimes also to any member of his or her immediate family). Chapter 21 reviews such Employee Counselling Services.

21   COUNSELLING SERVICES

The viewpoint mentioned at the end of Chapter 19, that in-company counselling services pay off in purely commercial terms, has been adopted by a growing number of UK companies, though it remains a trickle compared with the 4000-plus American companies who operate what are usually called Employee Assistance Programs.

It may be that, in the future, the informal and semi-formal counselling carried out by the managers, work colleagues and others who are addressed by this book will increasingly flourish in the context of such formal in-company counselling services. Their structure and operation would warrant a separate book. Here I have sifted down some of the relevant information under four headings.

■ ■ ■ ■

BACKGROUND

Historically, the original pressures behind the establishment of employee counselling services in the United States were linked to three things.

☐ The *first* was legislation which held the employer responsible not only for physical safety at work but also for what might be termed emotional damage, especially where that was construed as leading to catastrophic effects in terms of illness or death.

☐ The *second* was the incidence of alcoholism and drug abuse, which were calculated to be costing American industry quite astronomical sums.

☐ The *third* was the reaction of health insurance companies who, in response to the dramatically increased benefits they were forced to pay out, attempted to control the situation by correspondingly higher group insurance premiums and more stringent exclusion clauses. At the same time, they were willing to modify this tougher approach for companies which ran an employee counselling programme.

How much of this background is, or may become, critical in other countries, readers may judge for themselves. In the UK, those who have to deal with alcohol and drug abuse on a daily basis maintain that these are problems of far greater significance than employers are aware of or, perhaps, willing to admit. A current DHSS document estimates that 14 million working days per year are lost to British industry through excessive drinking, simply in terms of attributable absences.

It seems also to be relevant that the largest private medical insurance firms in Britain are already beginning to manipulate the terms and conditions of group and company schemes precisely to protect themselves against mounting claims for alcohol/drug abuse and associated psychiatric treatment.

New factors

Meantime, two other factors have served to foster the emergence of employee counselling services, and both are relevant to virtually every industralized nation.

☐ The economic recession worldwide has put many companies under pressure to reduce and/or redeploy their workforce, and at the same time to involve themselves much more in people's welfare. Again, companies are increasingly obliged for purely commercial reasons to take a longsighted view of manpower requirements, to handle redundancies in a more positve manner, and to take steps to attract the key individuals they wish to retain, in the face of competition and diminished company loyalty.

A handful of organizations, including one or two with a reputation for far-sighted personnel policies, now have a dedicated career counsellor whose task is to force managers and key technicians, from the very beginning of their employment, to think in the long-term about their working life, to warn them that the more common pattern may well be two or more careers – but that the company will give them every assistance with such transitions. No secret is made of the fact that this approach also serves the organization, in giving it more control over the middle-management bulge which can clog its development and promotion arteries.

☐ We are currently being deluged with evidence of the negative effects of *stress* on the grand scale, arising from the pressures, pace and fluctuations of modern life. Serious estimates of the size of the problem produce figures of such proportions that one is hard put to register the full import. In the UK, for example, 30 million working days per annum of *certified* absence have been recorded as due to what is officially termed "psychoneurosis". A study in one public sector group found that up to 30 per cent of the population was suffering from some minor psychiatric disorder, and a year later that only half had recovered. Some studies attempt to extrapolate for a mountain of similar data in order to estimate the total cost to the country, perhaps to quantify it in sheer monetary terms, and again even the most conservative statistics beggar the imagination.

As rather tartly noted by one observer, the stress phenomenon has become something of a bandwagon, and the accelerating awareness of it has been outstripped only by the rapidity with which some people have become experts in the field. From the proliferation of writing and experience, however, some sediment of received wisdom is beginning to emerge about the nature of stress in general, about the need for the organization to recognize and change procedures or environments which are unnecessarily stressful; finally, about the need for additional counselling services, since it is quite clear that reaction to stress factors is a highly individualistic and personal matter.

MANAGEMENT PHILOSOPHY

Whether or not an employee counselling service would be regarded as "just another management ploy", perhaps, or as a positive move in the right direction, would depend on the type of culture and relationships already existing in an organization. Which of the two it is might even be fairly apparent from the title. One company in the US calls it a counselling service for employees' problems. Another refers to its own service as brought into existence for "problem employees". The difference of emphasis can hardly be accidental.

However this may be, the numerous surveys of in-company counselling services are agreed that, to succeed, they must have the genuine commitment (not merely approval) of the top level of management. It goes without saying that, in unionized industries and organizations, the wholehearted and unequivocal support of unions and staff associations is equally necessary.

Such surveys, covering between them some hundreds of different counselling services, also note that successful ones are usually governed by the purely pragmatic consideration that employees' personal problems are costly in terms of productivity; and that people cannot realistically be expected to check them in at the gate and pick them up again on the way out.

Finally, they note that although the impetus behind many good services is performance-related and quite hard-headed yet it is also humanistic, in that it regards people as working not only for extrinisic motives (reward and punishment) but also for intrinsic satisfactions derived from work itself, from the environment, from friendships. Thus, the counselling service is seen as enhancing and restoring people rather than coercing or correcting. It works best when it is inspired by the twin motives that it is both humanitarian and cost-effective.

> "Many of our staff", said the building society manager, "spend most of their working lives sitting next to a pile of cash. In practice it isn't too difficult for some of them to 'borrow' a hundred quid from time to time. Now I'd rather we had a confidential counselling service for them, so that when the temptation arises (as it inevitably will) and they happen to be in a temporary financial bind, they won't do something which will probably be detected in the end and will automatically lose them their job."

SCOPE AND STYLE

The varieties of employee counselling services are virtually infinite. One segment of a huge engineering combine has a workforce of 120,000 and a counselling service manned by 127 individuals, all full-time employees of the company and available 24 hours a day, seven days a week. The service has an independent annual operating budget of $1.3 million.

Another company, this time in the UK and in the financial services sector, a subsidiary of a North American parent, has no internal counsellor. Employees go to a designated member of the personnel department who refers them straight to an outside commercial agency, psychiatrically oriented, which make an initial diagnosis, will see the individual for a maximum of five visits (without further payment) or where appropriate refer him or her to an in-patient drug or alcohol rehabilitation hospital. The costs are borne directly by the group's corporate (worldwide) medical insurance.

A third example is that of a UK newspaper group which has appointed a single counsellor, who makes a point of walking around the various offices and plant. He is approached on a number of confidential matters, may take up some three or four of them per week for more private discussion, and where necessary will refer them for specialized help.

The difference in scope between the three instances is enough to show that, though the impetus behind all three may be similar, an employee counselling service can take on almost any form. Indeed, experts in the matter insist that each company needs to work out its own unique formula. About the only aspects which are fairly constant are:

☐ The range of problems accepted is not limited. Even those services which started on a narrow base (alcohol, drug, financial, legal problems) have gradually evolved into the characteristic "broadbrush" service, where *any* kind of issue which is troubling the employee may be brought up.

☐ The typical performance-related impetus behind the setting up of the service usually means that union officials, supervisors and so on are given additional training in confronting performance issues and in referrring appropriately to a counsellor.

☐ If only because of the danger of a mistaken initial evaluation, but also as back-up, support and supervisory resource, most company counselling programmes use the services of one or more professionals, in-house or external.

COSTS AND BENEFITS

Results from employee counselling services, as quoted in published reports, are (perhaps naturally) positive, but they are sufficiently clear and universal to be worth looking at.

The *benefits* are assessed in various ways. One company, for example, assigned some 90 employees to a trial four-month period of counselling, among them an "at risk" group who were proposing to leave the organization for one reason or another. At the end of the period only five had left and even after two years half of them were will with the company.

This is neither a typical situation nor evaluation procedure. criteria are normally more general, and set against these, both individual organizations and broader independent surveys typically report 50 per cent improvement in terms of absenteeism, tardiness, accidents and injury, medical visits, sickness benefits, surgical costs, disciplinary actions and terminations.

They also often cite intangible benefits such as better public relations (both internally and externally), improved recruitment efforts (because of the company's better image), reduced interpersonal conflicts, and a more favourable, improved image of unions and management. Such surveys usually report strong support for the service; and an increasing use of it, with only small minorities indicating reservations. These are usually expressed as doubts about the true confidentiality of the service and concerns that using it might subsequently damage the individual's career.

The *costs* of employee counselling services, apart from the obvious ones of counsellors' salaries or the fee paid to an outside agency, arise from the additional supervisory training which may be required and the information, materials, documentation and presentations necessary to introduce and sustain it. A rough estimate of what this involves has been put at about $25.00 per year per employee in the total workforce, where the population is relatively large, say, above 1000. Some smaller companies have been able to reduce costs by forming a consortium with other local organizations, with whom they are able to share some of the overheads.

In calculating the *cost-benefit ratio,* it is generally acknowledged to be extremely difficult to quantify in precise terms the advantages and savings which accrue from reduced absenteeism, tardiness, training and recruitment costs, and so on. The most conservative estimates reckon the benefit-to-cost ratio to be in the region of two and a half to one, the more optimistic at as much as ten to one.

EPILOGUE

The setting up of counselling services *within* and *by* the organization is an appropriate note on which to end.

Counselling in itself involves a particular kind of personal relationship between the client and the counsellor. It demands care to preserve this relationship in the context of the organization, which is a third and interested party. From the above it will be clear that the necessary delicate balance between the organization's needs and the individual's has in a great many cases been successfully achieved. It requires trust and openness on both sides: on the individual's side, trust that his or her confidence will not be abused, and on the organization's side, openness to the possibility that counselling will throw the spotlight on weak spots in its own structure and functioning which will need to be corrected.

This book is written to bridge the gap between professional counselling and management. I neither want organizations to see it as a Trojan horse which would undermine its requirement to produce results – on the contrary – nor, because counselling skills are so powerful, would I want them to become a tool of manipulation. Within the approach adopted here both employer and employee would seem to be adequately protected, and to have better chances of finding out what they want from each other.

RECOMMENDED READING

This is a short list of reading that I can remember finding helpful. Each of the items has suggestions for further reading.

■ ■ ■ ■

1. Some of the reading I am most indebted to, like the help I had from my own teachers and mentors, has so seeped into my thinking over twenty years that I can no longer distinguish the source. But anyone who has read:

Egan, Gerard (2 edn, 1962) *The Skilled Helper.* Monterey: Brooks/Cole.

will know the enormous debt I owe to him. There are two differences between his book and mine, one of them being that this is shorter. The other difference is in the examples: mine all relate to people in their work setting, where Egan's are more general. But anyone who wants a fuller version of the same approach should go to Egan's book, in its *second* edition. The third edition, which has appeared recently, is a turbo-charged version, which at first sight looks rather different and definitely more complex; it makes quicker sense to those who have graduated from its simpler predecessor.

2. The second major source of inspiration is the brilliantly produced BBC Radio 4 series of Francesca Inskipp and Hazel Johns. Audio cassettes and companion booklet, *Principles of Counselling,* Series 1 and 2, are available under the Insight, BBC Continuing Education label, 1982.

Perhaps more for professional counsellors the same two authors have a very good chapter, "Developmental eclectism: Egan's skills model of helping", in:

Dryden, W. (ed.) (1984) *Individual Psychotherapy in Britain.* London: Harper and Row.

3. Hopson, Barrie (1985) Adult life and career counselling. *British Journal of Guidance and Counselling, 13(1),* 49–59.

Address to write to: Publication Department, Hobson's Press Ltd, Bateman St., Cambridge CB2 1LZ.

4. An excellent book, now unfortunately out of print, is:

Watts, A.G. (ed.) (1977) *Counselling at Work*. London: Bedford Square Press.

A reprint has been mooted. Enquiries to:

The British Association for Counselling, 37A Sheep St., Rugby, CV21 3EX.

Membership of this association is open to all and their excellent monthly journal, *Counselling,* is full of useful articles and information.

INDEX